Arise: Sir Terry Wogan

Emily Herbert

16
EasyRead Large

Copyright Page from the Original Book

Published by John Blake Publishing Ltd,
3 Bramber Court, 2 Bramber Road,
London W14 9PB, England

www.blake.co.uk

First published in paperback in 2006

ISBN 1 84454 297 1
ISBN 978 1 84454 297 0

British Library Cataloguing-in-Publication Data:

A catalogue record for this book is available from the British Library.

Design by www.envydesign.co.uk

Printed in Great Britain by

1 3 5 7 9 10 8 6 4 2

Papers used by John Blake Publishing are natural, recyclable products made from wood grown in sustainable forests. The manufacturing processes conform to the environmental regulations of the country of origin.

Every attempt has been made to contact the relevant copyright-holders, but some were unobtainable. We would be grateful if the appropriate people could contact us.

TABLE OF CONTENTS

PROLOGUE   i

1: ARISE, SIR TERRY WOGAN   1

2: BORN IN THE RAIN...   13

3: THE DEAR OLD BANK – AND RADIO TOO   36

4: BLIGHTY BOUND   61

5: THRICE-WEEKLY WOGAN   89

6: MR EUROVISION   118

7: TERRYVISION   146

8: WAKE UP TO WOGAN   162

9: TERRY, HIS CHILDREN AND GABY ROSLIN   184

10: THE TOGMEISTER RUFFLES FEATHERS   206

11: WOGAN: NOW AND THEN   222

BACK COVER MATERIAL   233

PROLOGUE

Has there ever been as ubiquitous an entertainer as Terry Wogan? The list of his radio and television credits is as long as it is diverse, the one common denominator being that the vast majority of them were hugely popular. It is all a long way from Limerick, the quiet and charming Irish town where Terry was born and grew up, and where his friends and schoolmates were quite unaware of the future success story in their midst.

Indeed, it would have been impossible for anyone to predict the path Terry was to take in life, for the secret of his phenomenal success is this: he is both utterly normal and utterly extraordinary. He looks and sounds like the man in the street, albeit it a particularly charming and witty man, but somehow he is able to project that image on a national scale, across the nation's airwaves. Terry is both one of us and part of a show-business elite.

And he has put it to very good use too, for Terry really has been there and done just about everything. It is difficult to know where to start in listing his achievements: as the annual presenter of the *Children in Need* appeal, which he also helped found, and the *Eurovision Song Contest* (when he's never seen on screen, for such is his fame that he now no longer needs even an announcement of his presence to let people know he is there) perhaps? As the eponymous host of *Wake up to Wogan?* As the anchor of that byword in naffness, *Blankety Blank?*

And, while it might have been naff, it united the nation. Back in the late 1970s and early 1980s, there were some Saturday nights when almost half of Britain sat down to watch Terry, in his kipper tie and wide-lapelled suit, and wielding that ludicrous microphone, allowing his studio guests to indulge in innuendo as he gazed on benignly, keeping the more raucous element in order. He has been part of the fabric of the nation for a long, long time.

Funnily enough, given his starry existence, Terry's first job was actually in a bank – 'the dear old bank' – but he moved into radio after five years and has never looked back. His knighthood comes on top of a whole host of awards: in 2005, he was named Broadcaster of the Year at the Broadcasting Press Guild Awards, and in 1994 he won the Sony award for Best Radio Breakfast Show. He has been voted TV Personality of the Year no fewer than ten times by *TV Times* readers, and as far back as 1974 won the Variety Club Award for Radio Personality of the Year. Terry Wogan has been massively popular ever since he first started broadcasting: his knighthood is confirmation of more than three decades of having them rolling – or at least chuckling gently – in the aisles.

And then there are the programmes. Who could forget *Wogan's Island* or *Do the Right Thing?* Well, quite a few people, actually, but *Lunchtime with Wogan, Come Dancing, New Faces* and, of course, *Blankety Blank* are firmly embedded in the national consciousness. Others include *Celebrity Squares, Auntie's Bloomers, Auntie's Sporting Bloomers* and *The National Lottery Live.*

Best known of all, perhaps, was *Wogan,* the thrice-weekly early-evening chat show on BBC1, and that's before you even begin to consider his radio career, both before and after the start of the TV show *Wogan* in 1982. *Wogan* was on our screens so long that it became a part of the national consciousness. Everyone born before 1975 has at least some remembrance of it, if not of some particular show that stayed in the mind. In short, Terry Wogan is a man for all seasons, capable of turning his hand to almost any kind of presenting on television and capable of giving it all the inimitable Wogan touch.

But, currently at least, it is his radio show that is winning him the most plaudits. Radio 2 might not be cool, but it is massively popular and that is largely down to Terry himself. He is modest about the acclaim he receives. 'There's a bit of fuss being made now,' he conceded in an interview before the knighthood was announced. 'But I've been there before as far as radio and television is concerned and I know that it's not an ever-ascending curve. Radio 2 will eventually level off and, when it begins to lose listeners, well, I have to get off the beach before that happens. It's a matter of timing. Just before the tide recedes. There's always a time to stop. *Wogan* was the only thing I didn't time right. And I didn't because I was earning so much money from it. So, instead of following my instinct, which I'd always done before, in *Come Dancing* or *Blankety Blank,* and stopping it when I thought I'd done enough, I let it go on for a year, or two years, too long.'

That is not the kind of remark that will thrill the bosses at Radio 2, who are well aware these days of what they have in their star, and have no desire at all for him to quit. But it is very definitely Terry's philosophy now. The very odd failure in his life, such as the time when *Wogan* went off air – and the programme was actually one of his biggest successes; the only problem was, as he himself admitted, that it went on for too long – has taught Terry both that nothing lasts for ever and that you shouldn't get too worked up by success because it doesn't last. It is a straightforward quality that marks him out from hordes of younger and more arrogant colleagues, and it derives from the simple fact that he's seen it all before.

Talk of leaving and retirement aside, Terry's phenomenal experience has played a huge part in putting him where he is today. Another element often forgotten in our youth-obsessed culture is that the very young may have a great deal of energy, but the older person actually knows what he or she is doing. There is not a problem that Terry has not experienced on air at some time, which means he can cope while others are left floundering. He is the consummate professional, always in charge of the proceedings and always knowing how to react.

And, crucially, he has never believed in his own publicity. In early 2005, when it emerged that *Wake up to Wogan* had gained more than 400,000 listeners in the previous three months, his response was typical. 'The thing to remember about listening figures is that, if you believe them when you're winning, you also have to believe them when you're losing,' he says.

'There's no such thing as an ever-rising curve. There was a time when I won TV Personality of the Year for ten years running and I decided to give it a rest, because I thought, When I lose, people will say Terry Wogan has been stuffed. So I retired and someone else won and people said, "Terry Wogan has been stuffed." We're delighted by these figures, of course. It's terrific and you can't help be flattered by it – but I want to know what the other 52 million are listening to!'

His long-time producer, Paul Walters, was also proud. 'Eight million is a fantastic milestone,' says Paul, who first worked with Terry in 1979 and, barring the *Wogan* years, has been with him ever since. 'There used to be bigger numbers in the old days when there were only four radio stations, but now there is so much competition, eight million is a real achievement.'

How much longer can this rising trend go on? Who knows? When listening figures reached six million,

Terry was adamant that it couldn't go higher than that, but it did – two million higher, to date. And there seems no reason why Terry's show shouldn't continue to bring in still higher figures. There are no inherent limits here: in many ways, Terry's been breaking new ground and continues to do so. And it's become a virtuous circle: the more his show is talked about, the more listeners it attracts. The more listeners it attracts, the more it is talked about. And so the show goes on, ever more popular, increasingly the only show that pulls in listeners in that particular league.

Terry continues to play down whatever that elusive 'it' factor may be that has made him such a success – and if it was simply a genial personality with a good line in quips, everyone would be doing it – but there's no question that it works. 'Let's be reasonable – they're used to me,' he says of the millions who tune into his show. 'Daily radio is about familiarity, having a friend at the other end of the wireless. I'm like an old hole in the carpet or the peeling bit of wallpaper. Those that can't stand the sight of me have long since decided not to listen. I'm probably the last person who can put his finger on it. All I do is open a microphone and speak. But you try to create a sort of club. You're talking to one person, not eight million, and you're trying to make that person feel part of the programme. You try to create an intimacy, a friendly voice they can lean on at that time in the morning. It's lovely to do. I just open the microphone and say the first thing that comes into my head.'

Simple as child's play? Hardly. But Paul Walters is in no doubt as to the qualities that make Terry such a success. Terry arrives in the studio at 7am (or 7.25am, according to which bit of the legend you believe) and it is not until he starts broadcasting half an hour later that he begins to look at all the emails that have been sent in. 'He doesn't look at any of the emails until the microphone is open because that would take away the feeling of spontaneity,' says Paul. 'He's a fantastic broadcaster because of his timing. He's not frightened of the pause or the mistake. He understands that nobody dies if we get it wrong. If you make a mistake, it's funny and he never struggles or panics. That's the difference between a DJ and a presenter.'

The other great secret of Terry's success, according to Paul, is that he comes across as the man in the street. He may be worth millions and own houses in several countries, but he talks about subjects that the listeners are concerned about. 'The car gets dirty, the grass needs cutting, he gets held up in traffic, there's nothing to watch on telly: he sounds like he's really in touch with the problems they have,' says Paul. 'And he really is like that – except that he obviously has an amazingly different lifestyle to the rank and file. He can't just go down to the pub, but he makes it seem like he does.'

And Terry does have a rather sumptuous life. He lives in some style in a large house set in its own grounds, beautifully furnished, clearly the residence of a man who has made his mark on the world. He lives well as far as the good things in life are concerned, although even here Terry's only vice is not that shocking – he enjoys a cigar after dinner, rather than pudding.

Terry also enjoys his holidays – he once recalled that someone sent a bomb to the BBC, and Terry was slightly miffed when it emerged that he was on holiday at the time. (The would-be assailant hadn't turned on Terry's radio programme and so hadn't realised that he was away.) Funnily enough, he has that in common with Chris Tarrant, the only man who could truly be said to be a rival in radio terms, and who also tends to go off on long breaks. In fact, as he himself fully realises, Terry leads a life far beyond the means of most of his listeners, which is why he is careful never to flaunt his wealth.

Everyone he works with admires his professionalism – no tantrums here – and another big Terry fan is his fellow Radio 2 presenter Ken Bruce. 'Terry's a self-deprecating man who's well aware of his gifts,' he said. 'He knows what he can do but he also knows it's not rocket science. He knows he's a good entertainer. He knows he's a brilliant communicator. His self-deprecation comes from his acceptance of the fact that it doesn't really amount to a row of beans in terms of great achievements.'

Except, of course, that it does. It may not be brain surgery. Terry might not have found the cure for cancer or even the common cold. But he does what it takes a very rare entertainer to do: he makes people happy. Certainly, some people can't bear Terry Wogan, and it is their prerogative not to listen to him, but a huge number of people are very big fans indeed.

And they are set up for the day by what they hear on his show. The car won't start, the boss might be in a mood and they've had a row with their partner, but, still, good old Terry is on the radio telling an awful joke. There is certainly some worth in what he does. Terry in some ways represents a form of escapism. There is a famous joke about the London department store Peter Jones: someone is once alleged to have remarked, 'If the four-minute nuclear warning goes off, I'm going straight to Peter Jones because nothing *really* awful could ever happen there.' The same is true of Terry. When he's wittering away on the wireless, it is very easy to forget anything that might be wrong about the world.

But how long will he go on? When the question is put to him directly, Terry's answer is typical: 'Until hell freezes over.' That is not, however, what he really thinks. Having slightly outstayed his welcome with the TV show *Wogan,* he is very keen not to make that mistake again, and has said so more than once.

'I'm too old to be doing this anyway and I wouldn't do it if I didn't love it,' he says. 'The fact that it's a success helps enormously. [But] people confuse longevity with merit. Look at Cliff Richard. Alistair Cooke, with the greatest respect, went on ten years too long. Jimmy Young left, which was a great pity. Ah, to be able to recognise when the tide is going out, when to get off the beach.'

Those words betray a rather sharper side to Terry than he is usually credited with and, indeed, to spend more than three decades at the top of the notoriously unstable tree that is show business requires more than a touch of the blarney. He knows his worth. He might give the impression of a small-town Irishman newly arrived in this country, but in truth he is very sharp. For a start, he has been very well paid for a very long time.

He is not afraid of reminding the BBC quite how many listeners he brings in and of demanding appropriate remuneration for it. He can be impatient and he can have a sharp tongue. One journalist who interviewed him once was rather taken aback to hear Terry being very unpleasant about someone else who had interviewed him – his persona may be immensely genial, but Terry is well aware of the position he has achieved in the world.

But Terry has a unique talent and, as observed above, one that the BBC is going to find very hard to replace when he eventually does decide to go. Terry is not unaware of that fact. Asked about up-and-coming talent, his reply was telling. 'I like Jonathan Ross. Ant and Dec are great little fellas,' he says. 'But there are a lot of people – I won't name names – who you do think: Why have they been given a long-term contract?

'They buy up people who've made it on a minor channel and expect them to make it on a major channel. You hope that people will emerge, but it's so difficult to produce anything popular nowadays. Universal appeal is a thing of the past. I mean, not even the *Eurovision Song Contest* is watched by everybody.' That was typical Terry – a very searching insight lightened at the end by a quip.

But then, of course, Terry came up the hard way. In these days of *Big Brother,* when celebrity, despite the lack of any discernible talent, seems achievable overnight, it is easy to forget that some people really had to work to get to where they are today. Terry didn't even start in radio, as many other well-known faces have done, and, when he got there, his initial assignments were to read farming reports in the middle of the night. It was a long time before he got to the glitzier aspects of his profession, and longer still before he started to become really famous. But, by starting at the bottom, he was able to learn his craft as he went along. It is what makes him the broadcaster he is today.

For all the modesty and self-deprecation, he also has a very good sense of his own position within the BBC. As he himself later said, he stayed with *Wogan* so long because he was being paid so much money. And, while he may not take himself or his job too seriously, he is well aware that not everyone can do it and is justifiably proud of where he is now.

Then again, he is well aware of the side of his character that does take itself too seriously and that is determined to hold on to the niche he has carved out for himself. In an episode of *Bob Martin,* the serious television drama of the mid-1990s starring Michael Barrymore as a showman, Terry played a sort of ominous version of himself – a steely-eyed and utterly ruthless broadcaster determined to stop the opposition coming up behind him and to hold on to his position presenting *Eurovision.* It was not the real Wogan, but it displayed a certain amount of self-deprecation combined with self-awareness to play a darker version of himself. No one can poke fun at Terry, because he's already got there one step before them. But, then again, he does it so cleverly that self-deprecation turns into what looks remarkably like self-defence.

Terry has appeared as himself in a number of fictional dramas, but this was one of the rare occasions when he was called upon to do some real acting. It provided an intriguing glimpse into what might have been an alternative career. His acting abilities, incidentally, should come as no surprise: as a young man living in Dublin, he was a member of an amateur dramatics group. It's fair to say that he enjoyed performing from very early on.

Not that Terry is too enamoured of the state of television today, especially reality TV, which he absolutely loathes. 'They can only go one way with that. It's got to get seamier and seamier. Eventually, we'll end up with soft porn,' he said.

Terry has a slightly moralistic, old-fashioned side to him, but, as his listeners feel the same way, this chimes with their thoughts. Here is another of the many reasons for his success, for, while he might not espouse the wildly fashionable, he does have his finger on what the country is really thinking. Does the majority like what television has become? Almost certainly not.

Terry was slightly flabbergasted to have interviewed a reality-TV star himself, a woman who was actually a pre-operative transsexual (that is, a man). This interviewee was being presented in a television show as a great prize to a group of men competing for his/her favours who were unaware of his/her real identity. It caused quite a storm at the time, not least because there were worries that the men would become enraged when they learned what was really going on.

The show was called *There's Something About Miriam*, and Wogan gave it his own unique take. He might have had to interview the woman (or man), but he certainly wasn't going to pretend that he approved. The combination of sexual provocation and the surgeon's knife was almost too much for him: Terry gave the impression that he could scarcely credit the world in which he now lived. 'It's called *I'm Miriam, Come and Get Me* or something,' he said. 'How low can you go? *Footballers' Wives!* I've never seen anything like it! *Nip/Tuck!* It's got nothing to do with plastic surgery – it's all about bonking. But perhaps I am an old fart...'

If he is, then so is a good percentage of the rest of the population. For Terry is not alone in loathing reality television, in bemoaning falling standards and in hankering after a kinder, gentler past – a good many other people do so too. And perhaps that is the real secret of his success: he provides a link between the Britain today and a Britain that was not as rough and not as coarse as it so often seems to be now.

And then he is also a good, old-fashioned pro. There is no starry behaviour from Terry, no outrageous demands. He doesn't really take to that kind of celebrity either: his is very much the world of the golf course, the large house near Ascot and dinner with his wife, rather than A-list parties, the Met Bar and staggering home in the early hours. It's not just his age: Terry's always been like that. He had a decent, middle-class upbringing that instilled certain standards in him, and that's the way he continues to live, even now.

Terry's family is by far the most important aspect of his life. He adores his wife and children and, when his middle child, Mark, had some problems with drug taking, his father was there to support him through the drama. The family are extraordinarily close: the children clearly dote on their parents as much as their parents do on them. That, more than anything else, is a testament to Terry's life: these days, to become famous and have your children still love you is a noteworthy achievement indeed.

As Terry is the first to admit, he has been fortunate. Many a talented person gets chewed up and spat out of the merciless world that is show business: there's no guarantee that able performers will, by virtue of their ability, go on to make the grade. But Terry has been prepared to take risks and, despite the cosy image, some of his work has been groundbreaking. Before him, no one had done a thrice-weekly chat show on television, at least not in this country.

Nor is his radio show quite as comfortable as the nonlistener imagines: there are times when Terry proves to have an incisive tongue. But, as George Bush senior once remarked, 80 per cent of success is just showing up. It can safely be said that Terry's certainly done that.

But, whatever the secret of his success, Terry – or rather Sir Terry – looks set to be around for some time to come. His popularity is higher than ever, he shows no signs of slowing down and the people who run Radio 2, as well as his vast fan base, are desperate for him to stay. It is a world away from where he originally came from – a quiet little Irish town called Limerick.

1

ARISE, SIR TERRY WOGAN

It was a cold December morning in London but inside Buckingham Palace there was a distinct air of anticipation. Her Majesty Queen Elizabeth II was about to create a new Knight of the Realm, a knight who was not only one of the most popular entertainers in Britain, but also undeniably one of the greatest broadcasters of his generation. It was, of course, Terry Wogan and he was unique in that his knighthood was actually a double honour. Terry, who was born in Limerick, by now had dual nationality, which meant that he was going to be both an Honorary Irish Knight à la Bob Geldof and a straightforward English one, too.

'I'm an Honorary Knight and a Knight,' said a delighted Wogan. 'I've got two badges – it means my wife can use the title of Lady. I'm surprised, that would be the first reaction, and delighted. It's a great honour. As an Irishman I'm doubly honoured to receive this.'

Some months previously when the honour had first been announced the verdict was almost unanimous: this was one knighthood that was thoroughly well deserved. Not only was Terry a massively popular entertainer, but through Children in Need he had done a huge amount for charity, too. And his career, which encompassed both radio and television, stretched back decades. Just about everyone under the age of 55 had grown up listening to, or watching, Wogan in some form or another – he was part of the national tapestry, and now he was being rewarded for his pains.

On the day itself, dressed in a black morning suit with grey pinstripe trousers, Terry was accompanied by his wife Helen and sons, Alan and Mark, and revealed that the Queen herself was a 'TOG' – one of Terry's old geezers or gals. 'She's one of the TOGs, although anybody who calls her that would be very foolish,' he said. 'You might get your head taken off. Although now it's STOGs – Sir Terry's old geezers and gals.'

But then it should be no surprise that the Queen enjoyed listening to Terry, for so did millions of her subjects. A master of the art of self-deprecation, utterly unflappable and with the sort of geniality that has made him the equivalent of the nation's favourite uncle, Wogan is one of those rare entertainers who have brought nothing but happiness to people throughout their lives. Ascribing his success to 'clean living and plenty of roughage', he has gained his place in the nation's hearts from an early start as a Radio 1 DJ, through a plethora of television shows to his current slot, *Wake Up With Wogan,* on Radio 2 in the morning.

It is a very long way from where he first began. Terry Wogan was a jolly little boy but there was nothing in his childhood that pointed to the fact that one day he would rule the airwaves. For the truth is that he is now in an unassailable position. There is no one else who can delight the nation with the odd strategic pause, a hint of a raised eyebrow or a perplexed look that just touches the spot. Terry even manages to look quizzical when you can't see him – be it behind the microphone on the radio or commenting, unseen, on the Eurovision Song Contest. A highly defined sense of the ridiculous, combined with the fact that just about everyone in the country has heard of him, means his presence is everywhere, even when you can't see the man himself.

He has achieved that other, much sought-after status of being a national treasure. Terry's appeal is universal: there is just a tiny bit of sauciness to make the matrons of the world giggle and redden slightly, but it never, ever goes too far. He comes from a gentler generation from the nation's current young: he will tease, prick pomposity, mock everyone including himself and might even indulge in the tiniest innuendo, but there is nothing you would be embarrassed to listen to in front of your granny. It's no secret why he is so widely loved and admired.

And, in these days of drink and drug-fuelled celebrity, he stands apart from the crowd there, too. With the exception of a brief period in which one son was involved with drugs, there has never been a whiff of scandal anywhere near him. What you see – a clean living Irishman with a longstanding marriage, a taste for the good things in life, and a sharply satirical tongue – is just what you get.

In many ways, that is greatly reassuring. These days we are used to seeing our celebrities become tarnished. Sometimes it seems as if behind every famous face, there is a drink problem, a family scandal or a nasty divorce. Behind Terry there are none of these things, and that somehow makes us feel better about ourselves. Celebrities are a gigantic mirror image of the society from which they spring: if we have faults, those faults are magnified to the nth degree in the lives of the famous. When we come across that rarest of creatures, a famous person who has led, on the whole, a contented life, it makes us feel we have the chance to live that way, too.

And there's the talent. Where that comes from no one, least of all the man himself can tell. He has the abilities society required at exactly the moment they were needed: television and radio were gaining a momentum in people's lives during the 70s that they had never had before, and needed a new generation of communicators to talk to the masses. It is not easy – you have only to look at a bad television presenter to see how difficult it can be to get the job exactly right, but this is not a problem Sir Terry has ever had to face.

Indeed, he's been at it so long and makes it all look so effortless that it's hard to remember a time when he hasn't been gracing our airwaves and our television screens. It is said that a really good actor makes it look easy and that is also true of a really good presenter. Wogan never freezes, never lets an embarrassed silence develop, never leaves a guest floundering on a hook. He says he's continually 'taken mumchance' – that is, speechless – but in truth almost nothing can faze him now. Live broadcasting on radio or television is one of the most demanding jobs for anyone to do well – just look at the hordes who get it wrong – but Terry makes it seem as easy as drinking a cup of tea.

Indeed, now he's the grand old man of broadcasting, not just a national treasure, but an elder statesman looking benignly over a more youthful, and less popular crop coming up in his wake, it's increasingly obvious just quite how good Wogan is. He himself has picked Jonathan Ross out for praise from that younger generation, but Ross aside, there's no one else who could possibly take his place at the moment.

Steve Wright is another popular Radio 2 stalwart, but his television career never really took off; Julian Clary is too risqè, and who else is there? In fact, the only person who has ever managed to compete with Terry Wogan when it comes to moving seamlessly between radio and television is Chris Tarrant, and he gave up his breakfast show well before Terry was ready to put the microphone down.

And sometimes Terry is so good it's almost unnerving for the people with whom he appears. He is so relaxed and so assured that any nerves at all on the part of his co-presenters or interviewees – for he is a game-keeper-turned-poacher and now frequently makes guest appearances on the kind of programme he himself used to host – are highlighted and thrown into sharp relief.

Then there's his Irishness. Terry has lived in the UK for so long now that, as he readily admits, it is the country that really is home for him; but for all that, those familiar Celtic tones, lilting gently as he speaks, bring to mind pictures of the Emerald Isle. You could be sitting in a small pub in the middle of the Irish countryside, swapping gossip and tales with an old friend.

In his lifetime the English attitude towards the Irish has changed quite dramatically to the extent that it is now extremely fashionable to be Irish, but right from the start, Terry has been a much-loved figure. His popularity is certainly not a recent phenomenon: it has been there right from when he first moved to England and that, incredibly, was nearly 40 years ago.

He is also unique. Irish entertainers have always had a special place in British culture but, to paraphrase the song, there's no one quite like Terry. Graham Norton is naughtier, the late Dave Allen more aggressive and the various participants in *Father Ted* more satirical. Wogan, however, stands alone.

Invariably good natured, battling against an incomprehensible world, he is an everyman figure, the little man standing up to the enormous machine that is the rest of the world: Terry is you and me.

And, unusually, his fans really do run from the very young to the very old, with some particularly ardent supporters calling themselves 'TOGs', or Terry's Old Geezers/Gals. Everyone, including himself, is a target for his wry wit but it is always meant to amuse, never to hurt. 'He's a kind of polite Billy Connelly,' says Robert Beveridge, a lecturer on the Media at Napier University. 'He goes into little reveries and paints a picture in his own world – but without the bad language.'

Indeed, contrary to popular belief, the foul-mouthed rants so beloved of some younger performers are actually extremely unpopular. As the BBC discovered when *Dr Who* returned to our screens, there is actually nothing so popular as family entertainment and that is where Wogan excels. He creates a sort of alternative universe while at the same time latching on to the little obsessions of his listeners and society at large. He acts as a kind of filter between the big events and what the nation really thinks.

On top of that, he has actually learned his craft. 'He's certainly got the blarney – he chatters away,' says Beveridge. 'And there's something to be said for people like Terry Wogan and [the late] Alistair Cooke, people who have been around the circuit a few times:

they have learned their craft and are not all the time trying to push the boundaries like Chris Evans. They are not always trying to be smart; they are comfortable in who they are and so you feel comfortable with them.'

John Beyer, the director of mediawatch-uk, agrees. 'There's a great renaissance in radio,' he says. 'A lot of people are tired with what's on TV and are seeking more wholesome entertainment on the radio. The last episode of *Wife Swap* wasn't very edifying and I think we've had enough of all the cookery, lifestyle, gardening and makeover programmes on TV. People like what's familiar and Terry Wogan is familiar. If you turn on his radio programme, you know what you are going to get – a mix of talk, laughter and music. It's all very light-hearted and that's what a lot of people want early in the morning.'

Given that 8 million people listen to Terry in the morning, Beyer is clearly right about that. And, like all the most popular programmes, Terry Wogan's has spawned a life outside the BBC: there is the TOGs website, where faithful listeners can leave light-hearted anecdotes on message boards much in the style of the great man himself. Terry is, in many ways, a comforting figure, which is partly born of his longevity and part from his immensely reassuring manner. To millions of people, he's like one of the family, there every day apart from when he's taking one of his legendary holidays to be chatted to or ignored, as the occasion demands.

He is also unique in that he manages to tread a path between humour and mockery without ever letting either get out of hand. Terry might tease, but he'll never hurt. He might pick on a subject, but he'll never forget he's broadcasting to the nation at breakfast time and so won't allow anything to develop into a serious rant. As the nation prepares to go out to work, he provides a comforting backdrop, setting the world up with a great deal of good humour for the trials ahead.

But there is a more serious man behind the smile. He himself is aware that his genial method of broadcasting is a world away from some of the more vulgar elements of today's media, and his popularity has soared as a result. 'The generation to which I belong grew up on a diet of radio and television that was universally acceptable,' he says. 'But over the past ten years, there has been a complete breakdown into niche broadcasting. Youth has become more assertive.'

Indeed, as culture generally has become more youth-oriented, so has the media that serves it. And there's a very good argument for saying the media is wrong. Youth-oriented shows, on television or the radio, gain absolutely nothing like the audiences they used to, and while that is partly because there are now so many different channels to watch, it is also because the country is ageing and simply not interested in what is being broadcast.

In many ways, it is astonishing that this has not been picked up elsewhere in the media. Terry, the country's most popular disc jockey, is 68. One of the best-selling magazines in the country, *Saga,* is aimed at the over-50s. A trend is clearly evident here, and yet the powers that be fail to notice it – apart from odd inspired moments such as *Dr Who* there is nothing to mirror the success of Wogan's radio programme. Indeed, when the odd attempt has been made to recreate his radio show on TV, of which more later on, it hasn't worked. The reason for this is because it has been combined with ideas aimed at a much younger audience.

But young people listen to Terry, too. This is the other element media bosses get so wrong. It is often forgotten that until about ten years ago the younger generation watched and listened to a lot of what older people liked as well. Yes, of course there were music and radio stations and television programmes that were meant to appeal to the young, but what was widely understood was that quality programming was enjoyed by everyone. Good detective stories, soap operas and quality dramas had widespread appeal, as indeed did the kind of family quizzes and talk shows Terry used to present. The idea that young people would only enjoy the loud, the aggressive and the vulgar would have been seen as deeply patronising, and the popularity of radio shows like Wogan's only serves to enforce the point that good-quality entertainment is enjoyed everywhere.

Of course, much has changed in the past decades, not least the number of radio and television channels now on offer. Where once there were four national television stations, and not a great deal more on the radio, now the average household is spoilt for listening and viewing choice. The days when half the country tuned into one television programme are long gone – cable, satellite and the proliferation of independent channels have seen to that. Radio has experienced a similar fragmentation: almost unending choice means listeners are that little bit harder to attract.

But when it comes to the remaining listenership, Wogan is winning hands down. Far more people tune in to him than his youth-obsessed rivals for he represents that much-loved form of entertainment – family entertainment – that elsewhere just seems to have disappeared. This misapprehension about what people really want stretches right across the media and so it is hardly surprising that one of the few presenters who is actually coming up with what the public wants should find himself in such huge demand.

Wogan knows that, and he understands exactly what's wrong with the other types of programme being broadcast, too. 'Radio 1, for instance, has deliberately set itself to appeal to the narrowest possible age group,' he says, in a thoughtful analysis about the state of radio today that prompted a foul-mouthed outburst in return from Chris Moyles. 'It seems to be a lad or ladette culture in which the opium of the people is football, everything is aimed at the lowest common denominator and the music is aimed at an age group somewhere between 10 and maximum 20.

'They're aiming it at the groin. It is probably reflective of the downward trend in British education. But there is a stratum of young people in Britain who are being educated and who do have intelligence – I wonder what they listen to?'

Chances are, they listen to Wogan, and have seen a great deal of him on television, too. And this again makes the point that current youth programming appeals to the lowest common denominator without realising that that is not necessarily what young people actually want. When the old guard was disbursed from Radio 1, did the listeners switch on the new generation of DJs and raise a cheer? No, they did not – they all switched to Radio 2.

Indeed, the only surprising element to Terry's knighthood is that it took so long to arrive, although it is not the first acknowledgement of what a popular entertainer he has become – he had already been awarded an honorary OBE in the 1997 New Year Honours List. But now he has the title he really deserves. At long last, Wogan has been honoured for his services to broadcasting and his adopted country, and now he really will hear those words: 'Arise, Sir Terry Wogan. You are a Knight of the Realm.'

2

BORN IN THE RAIN...

Was it a rainy day? History doesn't disclose. But in the last of the pre-war years, in the attractive town of Limerick, in the west of Ireland, the Wogan family was overjoyed. Their first son was about to arrive: a son who would one day become one of the most famous and popular light entertainers of his day. But Michael and Rose Wogan had no clue as to what lay ahead for their little boy: all they knew was that a much-loved child was about to make his way into the world, and so it was that, on 3 August 1938, Michael Terence Wogan was born in Mother Cleary's nursing home near the family home in Limerick's Elm Park.

'The Clearys were our neighbours and Mrs Cleary's mother was a nurse,' Terry recalls. It was typical of the small-town atmosphere in which Terry grew up that it should have been neighbours who delivered him: everyone knew everyone and they knew one another's business too. But, while some might have found that stifling, it did provide an utterly secure background for a little boy to grow up in: young Terry was able to run around and play with a freedom that many children are not allowed nowadays.

The absolute security of his early childhood is crucial to the man that Terry has become. The war might have been going on elsewhere in Europe, but Terry was young enough not to be troubled by grisly events in foreign lands: rather, he was able to run free in an atmosphere that was totally safe, for there was always someone to watch over him and always someone to make sure he was all right.

And this is what has made him what he is today. Unlike so many other show-business stars, Terry is completely content with who he is. He knows himself. He is happy in his own skin. He lays claim to a streak of shyness, but he is not insecure and does not worry about his role in the world. He is not crippled by self-doubt. There were no dark shadows lurking in the very earliest experiences of his childhood and that gave him a sound basis from which to expand and grow into his adult self.

Yet the atmosphere could sometimes feel restrictive, especially if, as Terry did, as he grew older, you yearned for a bit more freedom. For Ireland back then was a very different country from the cosmopolitan country it is now. Everywhere, even Dublin, was provincial: the Catholic Church ruled with a rod of iron and everyone was expected to know their place. The only thing that has not changed between then and now is the weather. Ireland's green and rolling hills owe their beauty to the wet climate and one of Terry's clearest memories of his childhood is the constant drizzle that seemed to accompany him everywhere.

It was, if not his earliest memory, at least one of the first things he remembers. He was 'born in the rain', he said. 'When people saw the movie *Angela's Ashes* they said it was ridiculous, all that rain. It was absolutely true to life. I was born with catarrh and the sinuses have stayed clogged ever since.' That is a slight exaggeration, but it is clear that Ireland's climate did leave its mark on one of its most famous sons.

Despite early years that could almost be described as idyllic, Terry has a curiously ambivalent view about where he was brought up. Unlike Frank McCourt, the author of *Angela's Ashes,* he grew up in fairly comfortable circumstances. But he was aware that not all his countrymen were as fortunate and he knows too that present-day Ireland can be a little bit sensitive about the portrayal of its past, as highlighted by the outrage when *Angela's Ashes* was published, because many people thought it gave such a negative view of the country.

'There's no need for the people of Limerick to be hurt by that,' said Terry of McCourt's book. 'That was all of Ireland. Poverty was endemic; some of the worst slums in Europe were in Dublin. Ireland didn't have any money until it pulled itself together in the 1970s. Wonderful, that old Celtic Tiger. I'm very proud of it. I think it's terrific.'

And it was the fact that Ireland was not a bustling cosmopolitan country at the time that has proven such a boon for Terry in his later years. For the Terry we hear on the radio today is directly shaped by the age in which he grew up. It might have been Ireland, rather than England, that informed him, but it was a gentler, more innocent age and it is that that Terry summons up on air. His various idiosyncrasies, his personality, his likes and dislikes, were all shaped in a provincial Ireland that no longer exists. And it is telling that we as a nation seem to favour Terry's view of the world over any other. It might have been provincial, but it is a land to which many of us yearn to return.

The Wogan family, although comfortable, was a modest one. There was nothing extravagant about the way they lived: it was not a time given to ostentation. Just a year after Terry's birth, war broke out in Europe, but, while the international scene was at best unsettled, the domestic one was quiet and unassuming. The Wogans, like so many other families of the time, hoped to better themselves but didn't aspire to the type of lifestyle the majority have today, let alone the one their elder son was eventually to assume. To live quietly and decently was all.

No one thought much of disrupting the status quo in those days: it was enough to work hard, establish a family and attempt to make something of your life. 'The point is, I'm the product of an Irish middle-class, bourgeois, conventional background' is how Terry himself put it. 'Nothing very exciting ever happened to me in my life except for the fact that I happened to stumble into radio and television.'

And that is the point. No one can be everyman unless they have had such an existence: had Terry had a flashy and international upbringing he wouldn't be the man he is now. Then again, now that he is rather more flashy and international than he usually lets on, he does tend to play up that aspect of his childhood. Terry may now be a multimillionaire, with a choice of homes in different countries, but he is very keen to emphasise that there was nothing unusual in any way in his background. He is still a simple man from a simple town.

Decades later, when he wrote his autobiography, he reiterated that his was a very typical existence of the time. 'It's the life and times of a fairly boring Irish youth in a backwater of a town,' he said. 'There's nothing really important in it. I never wanted to offend anybody.' As it happens, he did offend quite a few people when his autobiography came out, but more of that later.

Given that he shared a name with his father, whom he would refer to as 'the Da', Michael Terence soon came to be known as Terry by his family and friends. It was the name he was to be called from then on, but with typical self-deprecation he was wry about that too. 'Terry is not a name I've ever been tremendously fond of,' he said. 'I'd rather have been called something more manly – Rot Gonad, for instance.' It's difficult to imagine a Rot Gonad establishing quite the following Terry has, though – he might not have liked his name, but it is one that suits him and the life he's had.

Michael senior was a grocer or, to be more accurate, the managing director of the Leverett and Fry grocery chain in Limerick, a job he took on just before Terry was born. Rose was a full-time mother and, according to Terry, Ireland's worst cook. She was also devoted to her little boy. The couple were typical of the era: certainly not pushy or self-aggrandising and happy to play their role in the local community. That said, Rose was keen for her son to do as much with his life as he could. In later years, she encouraged Terry to apply for a job on Irish radio, which was a huge step away from the relatively safe and conventional life as a banker that he had been leading until then.

Speaking of his parents, Terry once commented that every relationship has a lover and a loved one. It was his father who was the lover and his mother the loved one. Rose could also be a bit sharp, with a wit and an impatience that her son inherited. Terry's steelier side – and undeniably it exists – comes from his mother, who was a hugely formative influence on her son. For all Terry's geniality, he can sometimes bite, and that is a direct gift from his mother. It is a side of him, however, that he keeps well under control.

The young Terry was on the whole a contented child. It was to be six years before his younger brother came along, which meant that, to begin with, he was to all intents and purposes an only child and so on the receiving end of an enormous amount of attention. Aunts abounded: there were Nellie, May, Rose, Kitty and Dinah, and a grandma, Muds, all of whom doted on the young addition to the family.

Terry was the object of unwavering devotion from all his family, which explains a good deal about the easy charm that has done so much to sustain him throughout his adult life. To be treated as the centre of the world in your early years gives you a confidence to survive all life has to sling at you: this may well have been the origin of Terry's engaging manner, as well as the confidence to take the risks necessary to get where he wanted to be.

He is aware of the effect all this attention had, to say nothing of the fact that it alerted him to a very different world from the one in which he was growing up. 'Until I was six, I was the sole focus of attention by my parents, grandparents and several maiden aunties,' he said. 'My auntie May, who managed a book shop, sent me supplies of new books and comics all the time. It was the comics, in particular, that made me aware of a life outside of the parochial society of Ireland.'

That was also the first sign of a stirring to move abroad. Terry may be as quintessentially Irish as a leprechaun, but he has actually spent most of his adult life in England and, from a very early age, he was aware that there was more to life than the surroundings, however agreeable most people found them, of Limerick. Asked in later years if he ever got homesick, he replied, 'Yes, I do. It's not so much I miss Ireland – I miss the Irish.

'I just occasionally miss the attitude to life that is peculiarly Irish. But I think, over the years, I've become anglicised, and I doubt if I could live back in Ireland, because I don't think I could stand people not going home after dinner. It's the Irish tradition of standing up from the table at one o'clock in the morning, then continuing the conversation until you get to the dining-room door at two o'clock ... then another hour in the hall before leaving as dawn breaks over the hills of Donegal.'

But that was all to come. Back then, Terry was a little boy, enjoying most aspects of his childhood and all the attention he was getting. Terry has more than once spoken of the fact that he was an only child until he was six. It is a key to his character: at such a young age to be established as the centre of everything does wonders for one's morale. 'I think that was probably an important factor,' he said. 'My mother adored me, and, of course, my father loved me as well. An only child has an enormous advantage. You are the centre of the world and you are confident and told how wonderful you are.

'I suppose I had self-regard, self-esteem. All the problems in the world are caused by people with low self-esteem. Hitler? Mussolini? It's me, me, me, all trying to assert themselves, and it's really an inferiority complex. We're all aware of our drawbacks, our inadequacies, that's not what I mean. It's not walking about in a cocky manner. Self-esteem is being happy with yourself. Not thinking you are wonderful or anything, but that you are OK. You can live with yourself.' It was an attitude that was going to shape the rest of his life.

There were also other aspects of being an only child that shaped Terry. The lack of a sibling in his earliest years brought with it at least some degree of solitude, which means that Terry is a far more self-contained man than is widely recognised. He has been ever since he was a child. He was often quite happy to be alone when he was young, relating that, when he was a schoolboy, he would come home and shut out the rest of the world by closing the garden gate. This might explain why he has eschewed the glitzier side of an existence in show business: throughout his working life, he has kept his professional and personal lives entirely separate. And it is not difficult to see which one he prefers: dinner with 'the current Mrs Wogan' has won out over showbiz extravaganzas every time.

'I've always wanted my own space, always been happy on my own,' he says. 'I'm not particularly gregarious, and that's probably ideal for being a broadcaster. I like talking to myself, maundering on.' He had fairly solitary times in the past too: one of his great hobbies was stamp collecting. 'I've still got my stamp album,' he says. 'I look at it occasionally and think, Look what a little anorak I was.'

Of course, he wasn't really: he was indulging in a pastime beloved of many a child. But he was also, did he but know it, preparing himself for the life that was to come. Again, this feeling of inner contentment, of being at peace with existence, was to serve Terry in a way he wouldn't have believed back then. If the boy is the father of the man and the boy leads a happy life, the man is unlikely to be a mass of neuroses. And Terry is not.

This has also led to a great deal of self-possession. Working on live television and radio always brings with it the danger of the proceedings descending into chaos, and a successful presenter must be able to keep his head when all around him lose theirs. Terry has that quality. It is very difficult to flummox him – a talent he has been developing ever since he was a child.

In this, he was quite different from his parents, who were very typical Irish church-going folk. Nor did they like to draw attention to themselves in the way their son would one day go on to do. 'My parents were shy people and the worst sin in the Catholic Church, after sex, was vanity,' Terry said. 'So how any of us came out of it with any self-regard, I don't know. But

I always had self-esteem. I think it came from being on my own for so long before my brother was born.'

Brian, Terry's younger brother, finally made his appearance on the scene when Terry was six. It was quite a change in circumstance: from being the undisputed centre of attention of his parents, grandparent and reams of aunts, Terry suddenly found he had someone else to compete with. But – and it was a big but – he was, after all, six.

His character had been formed, and Brian's arrival, while a shock, did not alter that. Terry had had so much attention all to himself for so long that he was very firmly secure in his own world. And having a little brother added a new dimension to life. Terry now found himself in the role of the older sibling, something he came to enjoy greatly.

Terry had a typical Irish schooling: his first school, when he was a little boy, was run by Salesian Catholics. 'I started school at the Salesians and then, when I was about eight, I went to the Jesuits in the Crescent,' he recalls. He was genial, inasmuch as a little boy can be, secure, doted on and ready to take on the world. In short, he was a very happy little boy, and has often spoken of his happiness in growing up in Limerick, a place where he had many friends.

There was, however, one element of his childhood, and life in Ireland in general, that Terry didn't like, and that was the Catholic Church. He has gone so far as to say his childhood was 'cursed' by religion.

'They [my parents] knew it was a lot of rubbish.' But 'there were hundreds of churches, all these missions breathing fire and brimstone, telling you how easy it was to sin, how you'd be in hell. We were brainwashed.'

It is an attitude that stays with him to this day, and so it is perhaps not surprising that he was not always entirely taken with his next school, a Jesuit establishment called Crescent College, which he attended between 1947 and 1954. Indeed, his memoirs about his schooldays went on to cause some offence among his erstwhile schoolmates and sections of the wider public.

Some of his memories were happy. 'Father "Snitch" McLoughlin was the prefect of studies,' Terry recalls. 'He was a stern disciplinarian. He was a great friend of the family and he was very good to my mother when my father died. A great school pal of mine was James Sexton, who is now a solicitor in Limerick. Others I palled around with were Bill Hayes, John Horgan, who is a very distinguished surgeon, Michael Leahy. Des O'Malley sat behind me.

'A great friend of our family was Gordon Wood, who would come fishing with my father. Gordon was one of my heroes, along with Paddy Berkery. Limerick was a good place to grow up in. I think it is better for children to grow up in a smaller environment. My children grew up in a bigger environment where it's harder to make friends and establish relationships. I loved growing up in Limerick.' Terry was free to run wild and play, something he took full advantage of.

But there was also a darker side to it. Schooling was very different back then from the way it is now, and so methods that were then standard, such as corporal punishment, would no longer be tolerated. Schools run by the Church tended to be particularly strict, and Terry, who was already less than enamoured of the institution, perhaps found that aspect of it made it all the harder to take.

As an adult, he has been scathing about the behaviour of the priests, writing in his autobiography that his Jesuit teachers used 'terror as their tool in the education of young minds'. He added that one priest took 'real pleasure in his work, obviously deriving spiritual benefit from offering your suffering up to God. The sadistic bit was that this was no spur-of-the-moment leathering.' This again was an example of the steelier side of Terry: he is not afraid to lash out at some aspects of society that he doesn't like – and his lack of concern about people's reaction was just as well, given the furore his comments went on to make.

In more recent years, Terry has become increasingly prone to ruffling feathers. His criticism of the Catholic Church and Jesuit schooling was certainly one of the more controversial attacks he has launched, but he has not been particularly kind about the BBC either. For all that he has avowed time and again that he lacks a rebellious streak, Terry has shown a tendency to lash out at institutions that might have constrained him or served him ill. Just as his experience of corporal punishment means that he has never entirely forgiven the people behind it, so, after rather shabby treatment on more than one occasion by the BBC, he has never felt the unconditional loyalty towards the corporation that many expect.

Certainly, Terry's contemporaries remembered their schooling differently. When they were published, his remarks caused an outcry: after all, the Church still maintains a firm hold on Irish society and many of his old friends and schoolmates were genuinely upset by his words. 'I think he may be exaggerating,' says Jim Sexton, Terry's best friend at Crescent College. 'To say it was terrifying is a bit much.'

Des O'Malley, who went on to become a leader of the Progressive Democrats, said, 'Sadistic is overstating it, as at the time corporal punishment was everywhere.'

And another old friend said, 'The priests who had to administer the punishment in school found it as distasteful as anybody. To talk of sadistic behaviour is an outrage, as is to suggest any of them took any pleasure from this. The Jesuits were the most honourable and just men you could meet and they never harmed anybody.'

Pat O'Connell, who became the first lay headmaster at Crescent College, was also upset by Terry's remarks. 'Terry Wogan seems to have done very well in life and no doubt this must be in some way due to the education he received from the Jesuits,' he said. 'They were and are dedicated to the students in their care.'

The Jesuit order itself said it was 'surprised and disappointed' at Wogan's words. 'It is a bit unfair to depict the corporal punishment at Crescent as sadism,' said Father Daniel Dargan.

Of course, times have changed so much that it is almost impossible to judge the school on today's standards, but what is clear is that Terry Wogan was not always happy as a schoolboy and remembers Crescent College as a place that instilled fear.

Other people supported him in this view, so he was certainly not alone in remembering a slightly difficult atmosphere in which to grow up. 'Looking back, it was sadistic,' said Len Dineen, who had also attended the school and was now a rugby commentator in Limerick. It was certainly a different kind of education from that which anyone would receive nowadays, but it had left its mark: it contributed to a certain restlessness and desire to move on to bigger things that Terry had begun to experience in his teens.

Crescent College did, however, give him a fairly decent education: Terry is a much more erudite person than he lets on. Asked in later life what the benefits of a Jesuit education were, Terry replied, 'Self-esteem and perhaps a little too much self-discipline. I was very good at Latin, although I've forgotten nearly all of it now. I can remember my Gaelic, though. It was a butterfly education – I think I could probably win *Who Wants to Be a Millionaire?*. I know a little about a lot. I was very well behaved – never did anything wrong. I was completely bourgeois.'

However, he remained unrepentant about what he had said. Saying that he was not surprised by the reaction to his book, he added, 'They got very annoyed over Frank McCourt's book as well, didn't they? I can only tell it the way it appeared to me. In general, my attitude and treatment of my time in Limerick is affectionate. That's how I feel about the city and about the Crescent. But there was corporal punishment and it was on the calculated side. Fine if people think differently – that's their privilege.' It was clear that he had no intention of modifying anything he had said.

And, despite repeating on many occasions that he never rebelled, Terry was certainly prepared to take a slightly different approach to life than the one followed in the past by so many generations of the Wogan family. For a start, there was his career – Terry has hardly worked in the most conventional of professions. And then there is this readiness to criticise and to stand up for what he believes in. Terry might not have been a rebel in the sense of drinking too much and running away from home, but he was prepared to challenge the accepted mores of the day.

That inner steel, that is only hinted at when he is doing his job on radio or television, but which quite frequently makes an appearance when he is talking out of working hours, came to light on another occasion when he was musing about his childhood. 'How anybody came out of Ireland with any self-esteem is amazing to me,' he reiterated.

'It's the Jansenist tradition of the Irish Catholic Church, you see. If the poor old hedge-priests had gone to Spain or Italy, they would have come back with a more liberal Catholicism than the ones who fled to France and picked up Jansenism – which was very rigid, very anti-sexual and very much along the lines of Thomas Aquinas and St Augustine. So what we got in Ireland was repressive Catholicism.'

What they also got, however, was the BBC. Life was most certainly not all about repression: in the early postwar years, British society was beginning to change and a great deal of that change was conveyed to Ireland and beyond via the BBC. In the 1950s, of course, the rebellion that was to sweep the world was still a decade away, but there was already a kind of anarchic humour afoot, one that was both enormously popular and influential.

Terry, like so many of his generation, grew up listening to the BBC, and it had a huge effect on him, influencing the way he was to think in later life. This is one of the reasons that Terry, for all his Irishness, has had a connection with Britain since he was a child, something he himself acknowledges. 'My sense of humour, while very Irish in lots of ways, is very influenced by the BBC Light Programme of the 1950s,' he says. It is entirely fitting he has ended up where he has.

That decade was the heyday of entertainment for all the family, so it should come as no surprise that Terry went on to become a scion of light, family-friendly (and therefore popular) entertainment, rather than the more dubious and frequently disappointing style of entertainment usually referred to as 'cutting edge'. As Terry himself said yet again, 'I've never rebelled against anything in my life.' But, while that might be, with the above qualifications, true, it is also the case that he views life at an angle. As listeners to his programme can testify, there is often a slightly surreal edge to Terry's broadcasting. He is not quite the entirely conventional broadcaster that he makes himself out to be, any more than he is the entirely conventional man.

But as far as rebellion in the traditional sense is concerned, Terry was never interested. It would not suit his laconic style. Even during the groundbreaking 1960s, Terry was still living a fairly conventional life in Dublin, albeit one as a broadcaster. He has simply never taken part in the massive upheavals of that decade or any other. In many ways, that might also have contributed to his enduring success.

Although Terry started his career in the 1960s, it is not a decade he is particularly associated with, unlike so many other performers who started out in that era. Somehow, Terry has always managed to convey the impression that he was always, simply, there. It helped, in his subsequent career in Britain, that he was largely based in Dublin at that time, but there is always a danger that, if you become too fashionable during a certain era, you also risk becoming dated one day. Terry has never been at the height of fashion – but then he's never been behind the times either.

Even before he reached his teens, Terry's interest in things English also embraced the type of books that he enjoyed, and this taste almost certainly contributed to his unique brand of humour. 'The books I was reading would be *Just William,* Jennings, public-school things, Wodehouse when I got older,' he said. 'I am a voracious reader.' That has certainly come out in his broadcasting. Wodehouse, in particular, can be seen as an influence: the great author himself once said that there were two ways of writing about life: to dig into it and become extremely serious, or to create a musical comedy. Wodehouse opted for musical comedy – and so does Terry Wogan.

As a youngster, Terry was also a big football fan. 'Limerick soccer was my life then,' he recalls. 'I remember watching Mick Lipper, the Collopy brothers. That team was my life for about ten years and I hardly missed a game at the Markets Field. I must say that I am very sad to see that Limerick are in the second division. How did that happen?'

But, back then, Terry was turning into a teenager in a hurry. He once contrasted his own behaviour with that of his father, pointing out that, while Michael was content with the slow place of Irish life, he himself was continuing to itch for bigger things. 'My father used to take enormous pains,' he said. 'He was a fly fisherman, and we used to go out on a Sunday, and the sun would be going down before he cast the first fly out over the river. What he really liked to do was tie the flies and get ready, and naturally this built up resentment in a young man.'

A turning point, although the young Terry didn't see it like this at the time, came when he was 15. Michael Wogan had been promoted: rather than managing just one shop, he was to become the general manager of the entire Leverett and Fry chain of 20 shops across Ireland. This necessitated a move to Dublin, something that initially caused Terry some pain, as he was forced to leave all his friends behind. But it was to introduce him to a bigger world – and to the bigger opportunities that came with it.

Terry enrolled at Belvedere College and, despite the unwanted change in his life, it was here that he first began to get an inkling of what the future might hold. He joined an amateur dramatics group, where he discovered that he liked acting and being the centre of attention and, even better, he was good at it. The seeds of a life spent performing were sown.

At the same time, Terry acquired a second love: his bicycle, on which he began to spend a great deal of time. He was not an academic boy by inclination, however, and these two pastimes did nothing to change that. This issue was beginning to be something to be considered more seriously. University was not on the cards – Terry was not overtly academic and not interested in prolonging his studies – and the time was approaching when Terry would have to think hard about what he was going to do with his life.

Moreover, he was beginning to discover another interest as well: rock and roll. By this time, it was the mid-1950s and the brand-new style of music now emerging was having a profound impact on those who heard it, Terry as much as anyone. Asked in later life what he listened to before the new type of music came along, he replied, 'Elvis Presley, Dixieland jazz, Doris Day, Bing Crosby, Frank Sinatra – that's what we listened to then.

'I wonder if young people today can understand the kind of excitement that the Beatles, the Rolling Stones and the Who generated for my generation. I would find it hard to believe.'

If truth be told, these days it's a little difficult imagining Terry himself being overcome by the then wild men of rock, but he was, after all, still very young and as ready to be influenced by new trends as anyone of his generation.

By the time he was 17, Terry was ready to become his own man. It was at that age that he finally lost his faith for good, something he later described as a relief. 'My whole life changed,' he said. But there was still a big question as to what he was actually going to do. He'd ruled out further education, and the idea of going into show business, despite his success in amateur dramatics, was simply not conceivable at that stage. But he had to earn a living and his parents were keen for him to get a steady job with a good pension as a prelude to marriage and children. As for Terry himself, he has always professed to have simply found his way by chance in various areas of his life. 'I never had any real ambition to be anything at all,' he said. 'I just kind of drifted into things.'

Even so, he was aware early on of the need to earn a living. His parents might not have been badly off but they weren't rich, and Terry knew that a job was imperative. It is an attitude that has stuck with him ever since. 'I did grow up with a realisation of what money was and how important it was, so I'm not naive about money,' he says. In fact, he's downright canny. Terry has earned a decent amount ever since his earliest days as a broadcaster, while for decades now he has been one of, if not the most, highly paid broadcaster in Britain. Terry is not content merely to be happy within his own skin: he makes sure other people appreciate it too.

He was also fairly frugal as a teenager, and it's another habit he has never shaken off when it applies to himself. 'I have no problems buying things for other people, for my family, but I do have problems buying things for myself,' he says. 'I couldn't walk into a shop and buy six shirts. I'd have to buy one shirt and then go back and buy another one in three months. I don't think it's meanness, it's just the habits of your life are formed before you get to 17.'

But all that lay ahead. The young Terry still had no real idea about what he wanted to do and where he wanted to go, let alone any plans to become one of the most successful and best-loved radio and television personalities of the age. And so he did what the great majority of the young men he knew were doing: he looked for a good position that paid well, with good promotion prospects and in a respectable environment. He found it, too, although destiny ultimately had quite different plans for him.

Rose, always ambitious for her son, was keen that he would do as well as he could, and so she and the rest of the family were mightily relieved when the young Terry came home with his big news. His future was assured: his chosen path had finally become clear, and he and his family could now stop worrying about the direction his life was going to take. He had got a job in a bank.

3

THE DEAR OLD BANK – AND RADIO TOO

So began a new phase in Terry's life: one that was expected to be a lifetime career and which actually lasted less than five years. Terry's first proper job was as a trainee clerk for the Royal Bank of Ireland, with a view to spending his life in banking. He earned the princely sum of £2 10s a week, which may not have been a fortune but provided the means for an independent existence, for it was also his first taste of freedom and life as an adult. His future seemed assured: this was the start of the respectable career his parents, and Terry himself at that time, had wanted.

It was a great relief all round. In those days respectability and a steady income were everything. As long as there had been any uncertainty about Terry's future, his nearest and dearest would fret: as it was, now everyone could relax. And these coming years were crucial to Terry's later broadcasting. Unlike so many of his contemporaries in show business, Terry had not started out by treading the boards. He had not sought stardom. He was an ordinary man doing an ordinary job, and he knew what it was like to take home a salary, pay rent, make sure the books balanced at the end of the month. It gave him a grounding in real life and was an experience he never forgot.

Ireland, like the rest of Europe, was changing. The period of austerity that followed the war was coming to an end and Europe was beginning to look forward to a brighter future. There was still no hint that Terry was going to become a major celebrity, but this was a time of opportunity, when an ambitious young man would be able to make his mark. And, although it was obvious to only a few people at the time, the hidebound structures that had held society together were beginning to break down. But Terry, like nearly everyone else, was unaware of the changes happening about him. He simply got on with his new career and began to blossom out as a young man about town. It was a happy time. Terry was surrounded by other young people beginning to make their way in the world who, like him, were sampling real freedom for the first time in their lives.

This was Ireland in the late 1950s, so life could certainly not be said to be wild, but Terry mingled with a crowd who enjoyed themselves and got on well with one another. By day, he worked; by night, he continued to cultivate his taste for the new music sweeping across the Western world. He made friends, played rugby, continued to participate in amateur dramatics and generally lived the life of a young man not yet burdened by responsibilities.

The fact that Terry was blessed with a sunny temperament made him even more able to enjoy his new life too. He was cheerful, good-natured and fun to be around. He had no complaints about life and had come to enjoy living in Dublin. Indeed, moving to the big city was the first step towards that larger move, leaving Ireland altogether, as Terry increasingly found the need to expand his horizons. But, as yet, he was happy to have a good job and a fairly secure life.

Besides, he enjoyed his work. It was not onerous and left plenty of time for socialising, and he and his fellow workers at the bank were not averse to getting up to larks when the occasion arose. They were young and carefree, at an age when life is not to be taken too seriously and the world is full of delights. 'I don't feel nostalgic, but I had a lot of fun there,' he said in later years.

'It wasn't difficult work and we had a jolly crowd. We used to fire wet sponges at each other across the bank concourse. There was a lot of that going on and a lot of what can only be described as surreptitious sex down in the vault. It was a more colourful life than working in radio.'

This was almost certainly a wild exaggeration, but those early years certainly had their moments. In his autobiography, Terry later described how he would hide when the 'pig man' came into the bank: the pig man was a local farm worker, who would deposit his wages from the farm and always carried a certain odour in his wake. So, indeed, did his bank notes. Terry got on well with the vast majority of the bank's customers and was easy and affable company at work and at play.

In the years to come, Terry would remember his time at the bank with enormous affection and humour. He recalled one occasion when, now one of the most famous broadcasters in Europe, he returned to the branch where he'd worked to say hello to his old mates. As he tells it, he was greeted by an old acquaintance as if he'd just popped out minutes earlier. 'There y'are,' said his former colleague. 'Y'know, you left the bank at the wrong time. D'you remember Mick Murtagh?' Terry nodded. 'And now look at him! Deputy manager in Timoleague!'

That might well have been Terry's destiny if he'd stayed. And his own take on what would have happened to him if he'd stayed is telling. In 2004, asked if he would ever retire, he said, 'I used to work in a bank, the Royal Bank of Ireland, and if I'd have stayed there I would have been retired five years ago, probably a smug man who had married a farmer's daughter. But, since I moved into radio, I don't feel that I've worked for a living, so I'm just going to hang on in here.' That last remark is not to be taken too seriously. Throughout his working life, Terry has protested that his job is not real work, while at the same time always appearing the consummate professional. It is simply part of the Wogan charm that he plays down any effort in what he does.

And he took very much the same attitude to his first career, breezily asserting that it was not too much like hard work. And that was how it seemed his life was going to be. Indeed, the life that would have been his could have been predicted from the start: marriage to a local girl, promotion, children and a wholly conventional life in a conventional career.

But life had other plans in store for Terry: after five years at the bank, he was to surprise everyone by moving to a completely different type of life. It was not, however, planned in advance. Terry did not spend his years at the bank plotting to get out: he did no more than see an opportunity for what it was when it arose, and take it. And, as history was to reveal, he was very wise to do so.

Not only was the move from banking totally unexpected, but it was also only by chance that Terry made the move that was to lead to his becoming a household name. Perfectly secure and happy in his job still after working at the bank for five years, he was reading the *Irish Independent* one day when an advertisement caught his attention. Radio Eireann, which later became the state broadcaster RTE (Radio Telefis Eireann), was looking for radio announcers and newsreaders and was inviting the newspaper's readers to apply.

By this time – 1961 – Terry had developed something of a taste for performing: he had taken part in a number of amateur stage productions and enjoyed it. Even so, until then he had not seriously considered a career in show business – after all, none of his family had a stage background and that kind of career had never crossed anyone's mind. Nor did it provide the kind of stability that was on offer at the dear old bank: show business is notoriously fickle and many a good man and woman have fallen at the side of what initially seemed a promising road.

But Terry somehow realised what an opportunity lay ahead. He filled in the form and posted it. 'And bingo, I got the job. Don't ask me how – I didn't lie!' It was quite an achievement, for, depending on whose account you believe, there were between 5,000 and 10,000 other applications for the job. Terry himself narrowed this figure down: 'There must have been about a thousand applicants. I think it was probably my mother lighting candles for me that made it possible for me getting a toe in the door.'

Rose had certainly encouraged her son to apply – a surprising move, perhaps, for a woman who had led an impeccably conventional Irish life until then. But she had always wanted great things for Terry and was canny enough to see that, risky as it was, a huge opportunity lay ahead.

And so it was to prove. Small, split-second decisions can change a person's life, and this was without doubt the case for Terry. He went on to take great risks in the future, to uproot himself and his family to the UK, to pioneer new styles of game shows and talk shows and to turn perceived notions of broadcasting on their head, but this earliest choice was the single most momentous decision he was ever to make. Had that newspaper ad not lodged itself in his consciousness, one of the most successful careers in broadcasting in the late 20th century might well have gone to someone else.

Terry is vague about what made him apply for the job. 'I don't know,' he said, when asked exactly that question. 'I was a great radio listener ... TV hadn't started in Ireland at the time, so we used to watch the BBC. Coming down the hill into Dublin, all you could see were these minor pylons, 40-to 50-foot aerials, sticking up into the sky, getting fringe reception.' Nor did he rate his chances of success very highly when he was called in for an interview: 'I don't know why I got the job, to be honest.' But get it he did, and so, at the age of 22 he was to start out on what would become his real career.

Terry approached the job with humour, later claiming that he somehow managed to convince the powers that be that he spoke four languages, and he was typically modest about his first efforts, saying, 'They should have binned me on first inspection.' But, as he sat at the microphone, something clicked. He had found the one thing he was really good at, he said years later, adding, 'Most people don't get that lucky.'

In short, he was a natural from day one. Terry Wogan, disc jockey, was on the verge of making his mark.

Some would hesitate to describe broadcasting as a vocation, but, in the case of people like Terry, this is very much what it appears to be. He is so good at it that it is difficult to imagine him doing anything else. Terry might have stumbled into it by accident, but he's a born broadcaster. In retrospect, it's easy to see that his personality and relaxed delivery made this the ideal field for him right from the start.

But back then there was no sign of quite what a success his career would one day become. And, although he was drawing an excellent salary in his new position, there was still that issue of longer-term financial security. His weekly income trebled to £17 3s 6d, but it was still a big risk he was taking, for the bank represented safety, while radio did not.

But the idea that he might come a cropper didn't worry Terry much. On the contrary, a slightly more reckless element in his nature came into play, which was exactly what was needed if he was to take advantage of the opportunity now on the table. Terry has taken risks throughout his career, and this was number one: embarking on this new career in the first place.

'It never occurred to me that I might fail,' he said. 'That's not a cocky thing. I think I'm probably too stupid to understand the implications of what I do. I have always been a risk taker with my career, though never with my family. I am a very conventional, bourgeois person, but as far as my career goes I have always taken enormous risks without really seeing them as risks.' It was an attitude that was to stand him in extremely good stead.

Terry's first-ever broadcast was from a studio in the General Post Office building in Dublin. It was a report on the cattle market, and that relaxed and congenial manner that was to serve him so well in the years to come was most certainly not in evidence. He might have been a natural, but it took him some time to get used to the demands of his new job. In truth, he was terrified. 'It was the most nervous I have ever been in radio or television,' he says. 'Green light goes on and you forget to breathe. Honestly, you think you're going to die. The roof appears to be coming down on you as you're struggling for breath.

'Oh! Murder! I was talking about cattle prices and I slowly went purple in the face because I completely lost control of my breathing. I felt as if the whole room was closing in on me. I've never had a feeling like it since. It was the most terrifying thing I've ever done. I've not been as nervous as that since. I could have suffocated in there.'

But it was done: he had made that all-important first broadcast (important as far as his self-confidence was concerned), got through it and lived to tell the tale. The worst possible reaction on either radio or television is to freeze; he had done neither. Nothing, not even hours and hours of live television for the likes of *Children in Need,* would ever cause him so much angst again.

Had he but known it, this was actually an excellent introduction to the craft of broadcasting. Most presenters find live broadcasts, on television at least, terrifying, but Terry has often said that his training on RTE made him able to cope with almost anything. Whatever crises occurred, he had almost certainly experienced them, or something like them, before. 'I always say that nothing that could possibly happen to me on British TV or radio can compare with the appalling things that happened on RTE ... It was a wonderful experience, great fun. You didn't know it at the time, but nobody cared. It had a liberating effect, it was terrific.'

And his new job was also liberating in other ways. Terry was again meeting a new crowd of young people, but these were not would-be bankers he was rubbing shoulders with, but would-be stars. Everyone was so young and there was everything to play for, and this ensured there was a certain amount of leeway to develop talents and skills. Youth bestows a kind of invulnerability: because life's disappointments and downsides have yet to occur, failure was not considered an option, not just for Terry, but for all his new workmates too.

Ultimately, years later, Terry would find radio constricting, but back in the early days it was like nothing he had ever done before. This was a world away from hiding from the pig man: this was broadcasting to the nation, even if, on his debut, it was only about what prices cattle were fetching.

But it certainly wasn't always an easy job. Terry's role came to be that of a newsreader and announcer and, in an interview about Irish radio in the 1950s and 1960s recorded a few years ago, he recalled quite how chaotic his working life could be. On one unforgettable occasion, he thought he was going to bleed to death in the studio, although, ultimately, he got through it.

'I was prone to nose bleeding at the time and about five minutes into the broadcast my nose started to pump blood,' he said. 'There I was, bleeding to death, and the blood splattering on the page, covering the words, and I'm brushing off the blood. In the end, the whole studio was soaked with blood and I came out looking like Lady Macbeth. Luckily, the bleeding stopped after ten minutes and I was able to finish.'

Again, uncomfortable and nerve-racking as it was at the time, it was excellent training for the future. Coping with the crises behind the scenes at *Eurovision*, later on, was nothing compared with this. Of course, it shouldn't be forgotten that this type of work did suit his temperament extremely well: Terry was never one to panic, whatever he was doing, and his inner insouciance fitted in completely with the chaotic side of radio.

But there were some high old times there – legend has it that on one occasion various RTE newsreaders tried to undress the female newsreaders as they did their job – to say nothing of some bitter disappointments. Terry says that the biggest regret of his career occurred in June 1963, after Radio Eireann decided that he should be the one to cover the visit of President John F. Kennedy.

It was an extremely prestigious role he was called upon to play, but, in the event, he was denied a view of the great man. 'I was selected to be one of the commentators on the Kennedy visit,' he said. 'Let's face it, everybody in RTE was selected to be a commentator then, because it was such a huge outside broadcast. But it was an enormously ambitious thing for RTE to do.

'Anyway, there I was on the corner of Dame Street in Dublin, and my job was to pick up the Kennedy cavalcade as it came round the pillars of the Bank of Ireland and swept past Trinity College. It was only to be a couple of minutes, but a couple of minutes of glory. But, as the car came round the corner, the president leaned forward and tapped his driver on the shoulder and suddenly the car shot by me at about 60mph. I had been sitting there for hours and I didn't even get a proper view of President Kennedy's face – it was a great blow to me.'

These disappointments apart, it was not long before Terry started making a name for himself. He was proving to be a natural in his new job, and for all the problems, such as nosebleeds, and disappointments, such as missing the President, he was becoming quite well known about Dublin. He was certainly nowhere near being a household name – that was to come later – but people were beginning to talk about him. A buzz was definitely beginning to develop around Terry Wogan.

He enjoyed this new status as a man about town. Nothing, they say, succeeds like success, and as Terry became increasingly well known he was increasingly invited everywhere, which in turn contributed to his growing celebrity. And, had he had a very different personality, this would have offered another opportunity to mess up, for an early taste of fame can often act as a catalyst to oafish, egotistical behaviour that finally becomes self-destructive. But that inner security and self-confidence saved Terry then, and ever since, from becoming yet another showbiz boor.

And it was as he was beginning to absorb this newfound status that he met the woman who was to become his wife. As he tells it, he would never have had the courage to talk to her had he not found himself to be a minor celebrity at the time. She was a beautiful girl about town and already well known. Terry was a boy from Limerick, but he was on the verge of making it big and it was knowing this that gave him the confidence to strike up a conversation. And that, as far as his love life was concerned, was that.

Terry met Helen at a party and was immediately struck. 'She was a very famous model, gorgeous,' he says. 'If I hadn't had a bit of success, I'd never have had the nerve to go across to her. Hel says there was an instant spark, and I remained sober, which is not particularly traditional. I drove her home in my Morris Minor with the broken passenger seat. I kissed her goodnight. She let me. Only a little kiss, it was an Irish courtship.'

Helen was, indeed, a name in her own right: she was a house model for Balmain. It was the first big romance either of them had had and from that day forth they were an item, although their courtship was conducted in a proper, Irish way, one which would seem totally alien to so many people now. There were dates, but nothing improper ever occurred, and the relationship was not rushed: it developed at its own pace. Terry and Helen were married two years later, in 1965. Neither had ever had another lover and the relationship flourishes to this day.

This bygone style of romance suited Terry, who looks with a certain degree of distaste upon the sexual mores of today. Like many of his listeners, perhaps, he believes a more old-fashioned courtship is a better way of finding a life partner than today's more frenzied approach. 'The idea that we were deprived of sex!' he says. 'Romance is predicated on the non-fulfilment of the sexual urge. The frisson of non-fulfilment is probably more exciting than sex.

'I'd be hopeless nowadays. Things are too confrontational; I could never take to promiscuity. I'm too fastidious. Anything used to put me off. Anything! Women think that men will take anything going. No, they won't.' Terry certainly didn't: his wife's beauty and poise have often been a talking point among those who have met her. Mr – as he then was – Wogan had got himself quite a catch.

Marriage to Helen, who, 40 years on, he still refers to as 'the current Mrs Wogan', provided Terry with exactly the sort of domestic stability he needed as he prepared to go out in the world. His career was taking off, but there was still a great deal of insecurity attached to his lifestyle and having Helen as a wife made it much easier to cope with any problems at work. She provided him with a comfortable home base from which to branch out and, to her husband's great delight, also turned out to be an excellent cook. Enjoying a good meal had always been one of Terry's favourite pastimes and now he had the pleasure of eating well in his very own home. So, for him, culinary prowess was a much sought-after quality in a wife.

And both of them were firmly convinced that this was it. Both came from a generation that believed that marriage was for life, and so they were fully prepared to make it a success, and, although any relationship needs to be worked at, the two were extremely compatible from the start. It has proven to be a good match. 'We're careful of each other,' says Terry.

'The things that we argue about are so small and inconsequential, like 'Where are my socks?' or 'These handkerchiefs are dirty.' We never shout at each other for more than ten seconds and then we regret it. She's a great cook and she's very kind, gentle and loving. I think she's the best person I've ever met. She would have been steadfast and happy and made anyone happy. I can't conceive of her not making anyone happy. We were never going to be separated. We were always going to be married for life.'

And that is the way relationships worked in those days. Divorce was still massively frowned upon in Britain, let alone in Ireland. Both Terry and Helen knew there was no turning back. And the great advantage of their prolonged courtship was that they had got to know each other extremely well. They had a great deal in common. Apart from finding each other attractive, they wanted the same things from life.

These days the two are so comfortable with each other that being apart would be unthinkable. Terry, as ever, plays it down. Asked if Helen was looking forward to his retirement, he replied, 'The present Mrs Wogan is a golf and bridge professional. She barely knows I'm there. I occasionally pass her on the stairs. I don't think she recognises me any more.' In fact, they are closer than they have ever been. The passage of the years, during which they have faced the trials every couple must face, has made them stronger than ever. Theirs has been an extremely happy relationship, and for that they have luck, as well as good judgement, to thank.

Two years into the marriage, however, tragedy struck. The two had been hoping to start a family and Helen became pregnant with their first child, a daughter they named Vanessa. However, Vanessa died in intensive care when she was just three weeks old. It scarred the two of them for life, to the extent that neither has been able to talk at length about what happened until now, and when Terry wrote his autobiography he devoted just three paragraphs to the episode. It is clear that the pain he felt then he carries with him still.

'I've been really happy most of my life,' he says, by way of explaining why he decided to write about his first-born child. 'I felt that I should write it because it affected Helen and I so much, although we never talk about it. I think it's important for my children to read about it because Helen and I wouldn't have discussed it much.' Indeed, he described how, when the tragedy happened, he smashed his fist against a wall, such was his grief.

It was another element in his turning away from religion. 'Your experience of life, your experience of the sheer unpredictability, unfairness and appallingness of life for some people,' he says. 'Then you look at your own life and how lucky you were and you think, There is no plan here I can identify.'

The couple eventually went on to have three more children: Alan, Mark and Katherine, all much cherished and a great joy to their parents. And Terry continued to pursue his career: after two years doing what might be termed a 'solemn job' at RTE, he decided he wanted to try the lighter side of the business and so moved across to become a radio disc jockey. He also began to appear on television, which contributed both to his gaining more experience and to the rise in his popularity, as he became increasingly well known. He was even beginning to catch the eye of the BBC in London, who got in touch shortly afterwards. Radio 1 was on air and flourishing – would Terry be interested in working for this brand-new station?

Yes, he would, was the answer. But they were not yet ready to offer Terry a good enough job to make him consider leaving Dublin and so he decided he would work for both RTE and the BBC. First, he presented *Midday Spin* for the Beeb in the mid-1960s and then, in 1967, the year in which his first son, Alan, was born, he started working for Radio 1. He was presenting *Late Night Extra,* for which he commuted from Dublin. It was not an arrangement that delighted everyone at RTE. As for Terry, he was clearly beginning to cast his net more widely.

These days Terry is rather amused that, because he is so closely associated with Radio 2, it is often forgotten that he actually started on Radio 1. Asked if he would ever take his show on the road, as in the good old days of Radio 1, he replied, 'Thank you for remembering that I was once a Radio 1 jock. Indeed, the way things are going on Radio 1 at the moment, I may well be called upon to return! I haven't the smallest intention of taking the show on the road, because of the state of [producer] Paul Walters's trousers.'

This uneasy state of affairs, broadcasting for both Irish and British radio stations, staggered on for a few years more. But eventually Terry began to feel that he had perhaps done all that he could for the Irish station. What had been liberating when he started out working for Irish radio began to feel frustrating: he wanted to be able to experiment more, to take some licence with his position, and RTE was not happy about that.

The station wanted a straightforward DJ who would play records and chat in between times, not a slightly maverick personality that might be difficult to control. And so tensions began to surface: Terry wanted to move forward in a way that wasn't allowed. Meanwhile, commuting between London and Dublin every week was an exhausting way to live and could not continue indefinitely. And so, for the second time in his career, Terry began to prepare himself for a big risk.

But it was two years later before matters came to a head. Radio 1 needed someone to cover for Jimmy Young while he was on holiday and Terry, who had become increasingly popular in Britain in the time he had been broadcasting on the BBC, was the person who was asked to stand in. But there was no long-term job offer on the table: just a few weeks' work. Terry decided it was time to see what the future held. If RTE would not give him the licence to broadcast as he wished, he was clearly going to have to find a more accommodating employer. And the BBC might just be the place to furnish him with the opportunity to move ahead.

He resigned from RTE and moved his family to England, a very risky undertaking, given that there was no assured future for him there at all. After a couple of weeks, he could have found himself with no job and no career, as RTE was very unlikely to take him back should anything go wrong, and it would have been a high-profile failure as well.

Nevertheless, it was time to go and when he left RTE for London, with only a six-week contract, Terry seemed unaware of the risk he was taking. But once again his devil-may-care outlook came to the fore. 'There was a lot of publicity in Ireland because I was an established name there and it never occurred to me that I could be going back with my tail between my legs six weeks later,' he said. 'I'm not a great one for failure. I'll recognise it. I'll say, "No, that didn't work." But it won't stop me.'

And although the Wogans may not have realised it at the time, they were leaving their native land for good. Terry had never had any particular desire to live and work in England, just as, before his big break, he had never imagined working in radio, but again he was prepared to go in the direction the tides were taking him. At that time, there was undeniably more opportunity in London than there was in Dublin: the BBC's radio coverage was expanding massively and the 1960s were in full swing. Terry might not have participated in some of the more outré practices of that decade, but he was infected by its energy as much as anyone else, and champing at the bit to do more.

And certainly RTE never seemed to realise what a gem it had in the young Wogan. Not only did his bosses not allow him free rein, but also they seemed to treat him casually, not valuing the talent they had growing in their midst. Terry was particularly upset when he was passed over as the presenter of a new quiz show that was introduced to replace another show, *Jackpot,* that he had been presenting.

'RTE had been planning a quiz called *Quicksilver* with Bunny Carr, but they never told me,' he said. 'That was instrumental in my saying to myself, "They could have treated me slightly better or told me what they were planning to do." It had the effect of making me look elsewhere and I went to work in England. [But] RTE gave me the opportunity to change my life. I owe it all to RTE. I'll never forget it – I loved it.'

It certainly showed his sense of self-worth. Terry was still a fairly junior broadcaster, but he was beginning to expect to be treated with a certain amount of respect. And, given that he was already feeling constrained at RTE, to have the sense that he was being passed over made him feel all the more aggrieved. Looking back, it should be no surprise that Terry decided it was time to move on.

He was harsher, though, on another occasion, when he was interviewed for a radio documentary about RTE, to be aired on that very channel. 'RTE never allowed me to develop as I would have liked,' he said. 'The system tried to turn me into a seagull, very little thought was given to expression. When I was offered the job with the BBC, I jumped at the chance because I knew I would be given every opportunity to use my abilities to the full. I always say that I would not have developed as a broadcaster if I had stayed at RTE because all the developments there, in terms of ad-libbing and freedom of broadcasting, did not happen until the eighties. It took 20 years for RTE to catch up.'

This was a forerunner of what he would later say about the BBC. Woe betide the institution that displeases Terry: like the elephant, he has a long memory and never forgets. It's a surprising aspect to his character. His is a sunny, easy-going temperament, but for some reason he finds it very hard to let go of grievances in the past. Apart from his schooling, though, these grievances do appear to be all work-related, suggesting that Terry was keener on developing a highly successful career than he usually lets on.

'If I hadn't come across to the UK, I wouldn't have had the same freedom to ad lib – to make it up as I went along,' he continued. 'That was the problem about early television in Ireland – it was scripted, it was tightly put together and it was run on a shoestring. Television was particularly difficult, because you didn't have use of an autocue. You were at the mercy of the director and you had to stand where the light was. Like an actor, you had to hit your spots and then remember what you were supposed to say.'

In later years, the BBC, just like RTE, would come in for some strong criticism from Terry. Again, it revealed a different layer under that geniality: modest he may be, but, if not allowed to use his talents to the full, Terry was not a happy man. And he was not afraid to speak out about it. Nor was he always prepared to forgive and forget.

But it was not just work that was on Terry's mind as this new phase of his life began. That 1969 could have been a difficult year for an Irish family to move to mainland Britain was something that Terry was well aware of. And he still has strong views on the matter. 'That is when what is euphemistically called the Troubles began, when the marches, which were so cruelly misinterpreted, started the whole nonsense,' he says.

'If they had been allowed to march peacefully, and people had been allowed the right to work, and not have their voting boundaries gerrymandered, and not been beaten up because they were one religion or another, and not been discriminated against. All legitimate complaints that unfortunately people didn't recognise.'

That, however, was a rare outburst. Perhaps because of his nationality and the year in which he came to England, Terry has tried to avoid politics, unless he's taking the mickey out of individuals, particularly in this field. 'Most Irish people, both North and South, just wish it would go away,' he says. 'All people want is to be left alone with their lives.'

Despite the politics of the day, in terms of his career it was time to make the next move. Terry had now been a broadcaster for the best part of a decade and was in his early thirties, a time when it is often necessary to make big steps to further a career. And he wanted a change, a new challenge. Throughout his career, he has managed to nip nimbly from one new venture to another. Apart from anything else, it has kept him from going stale.

But, all the same, it was a huge wrench. He wasn't just leaving his job: he was leaving his country to go to one where he felt entirely at ease but which was, nonetheless, a foreign land. And he had a family now: a wife and a baby son. But Britain was calling and

Terry was ready. It was time for Sir Terry Wogan to take the next, and biggest, step of his career.

4

BLIGHTY BOUND

The step was made, the deed was done and the Wogan family, which at that point numbered Terry, Helen and Alan, had uprooted from Ireland and settled in England. They were all looking forward to their new life, although with a certain amount of trepidation: Terry had taken a big risk in moving his family, given the small amount of work that was definitely on offer. But he had taken risks before and won, so there seemed to be no reason not to try it again.

The Wogans moved in 1969, in the middle of an era that was turning accepted modes of behaviour on their head and still to an extent defines the values of the society in which we live today. The old guard was on its way out and in this new, exciting epoch anyone could succeed if they had the right abilities. The old school tie was no longer a must.

London was awash with talented cockneys who now dominated the arts and the social scene, while the most significant popular entertainers of the decade, the Beatles, were working-class boys from Liverpool. Anything was achievable, anything was doable. You simply had to have the talent and the drive. For a young man newly arrived from Ireland, it must have

62

seemed like another planet, but it was one in which he was to thrive.

And it was an exciting time to be joining the BBC's new radio stations. Everything was still extremely new and untested, an ideal opportunity for a generation of young disc jockeys to begin to make their mark. Just as society was undergoing profound changes, so broadcasting was being turned upside down: above all, it was the start of a new emphasis. Before, almost everything on television and radio had been aimed at the middle-aged; from now on, there was to be a marked shift towards youth. And Terry, for all his unexcitable approach which now suits Radio 2's audience so perfectly, was in on it from the start.

In fact, while he now might be the face of Radio 2 and the middle-aged (the target audience having changed again) and while he might rail against the nation's obsession with youth, he was at one stage a beneficiary of that shift in style. Like the majority of people associated with the new radio stations in those days, Terry was young himself, with all the drive, energy and ambition that that phase in life can bring. And, for all his earlier protestations about being ultimately uninterested in actively pursuing a career, he was keen to get started. After all, he'd staked everything on this move to London and was very keen that his gamble should pay off.

And what a time to begin. The face of radio was changing fast and beyond all recognition. The revolution had begun in 1964 when the independent station Radio Caroline went on air, broadcasting from a boat off the English coast in order to bypass the legislation governing radio in those days. Caroline had been greeted with wild excitement by its young listeners, still revelling in the new style of music and broadcasting that was unheard of just a few years earlier.

Until then there had only been the restrained Light Programme on the BBC, which to our ears today would sound as if it belonged to a completely different generation, as indeed it did. The new music demanded new outlets and that was what was popping up now. Radio Caroline was not the only small, independent radio station revolutionising the hitherto genteel world of broadcasting. Radio Luxembourg, broadcast, as the name implied, from that minute country, was another of the new style of radio stations, all adding to the excitement of a new era in listening.

The very fact that these stations were broadcasting from outside Britain's coastal waters gave the audience an added thrill. Although the stations and the music they played were soon to become mainstream, at the very beginning, at least, listeners felt as if they were part of a new and exciting club. This was the age when the teenager came to the forefront, and the offshore radio stations had a frisson of something illicit about them. Just tuning in felt like an act of rebellion. What was more, the audience was getting used to hearing something new all the time in the fast-changing world of chart hits.

Initially, the powers that be were not at all pleased about the clutch of new stations that were springing up just outside the boundaries, beyond government control. There was an attempt to stamp on the new 'pirate' stations, in the shape of the Marine Offences (Broadcasting) Act, but the shift in prevailing attitudes to radio, mirroring the changes in the wider society, was too strong to be contained by legislation. A movement had begun that was changing the face of Britain, and broadcasting was swept along with it.

And so, in 1967, just three years after Radio Caroline had caused such excitement, the BBC conceded that, if you can't beat them, join them, and Radios 1 and 2 were born. In fact, at that stage, Radio 2 was essentially still the more staid Light Programme, not least because its listeners didn't want that much-loved station to disappear. The same year also marked the birth of Radios 3 and 4.

The two popular new stations, Radio 1 in particular, caused an immediate sensation and their launch itself was a piece of cultural history. But what is often forgotten these days is that in the early years Radios 1 and 2 were, at some parts of the day, one and the same – in fact, much of Terry's early broadcasting for the BBC went out simultaneously on 1 and 2. But, from the first, the all-important breakfast programmes were separate and set the tone for what was to come.

The big day was to be 30 September 1967. This date has always been remembered as marking the launch of Radio 1, so it is slightly ironic that the first broadcast to go out that day on the new channels was actually Radio 2, at 5.30am, when Paul Hollingdale went on air with *Breakfast Special*. Nearly 40 years on, this looks fitting, given that Radio 2 is widely considered to be the more successful of the two stations, especially where the breakfast programme is concerned, but at that time all attention was on the brash new beast in the jungle: Radio 1.

The big moment actually came at 7am on the day. Robin Scott, the Controller of the two stations, was the first to speak: he played a piece of music composed by George Martin called 'Theme One' and then introduced the new stations with the words: 'Five – Four – Three – Radio 2 – Radio 1 – Go!' And with that Tony Blackburn came on air on Radio 1, playing 'Flowers in the Rain' by the Move. It was not yet a totally independent service: Radio 1 broadcast for just five hours and 35 minutes on its first day, mainly because of lack of funds and restrictions on needletime. For the rest of the time, it linked up with Radio 2.

But the revolution had begun and it was in this febrile atmosphere that Terry had first started to broadcast for the BBC. It was a wildly exciting time, made all the more so by the fact that there was still heavy rivalry from its competitors. Radio Caroline had managed to survive the Marine Offences Act and, unlike Radio 1, was broadcasting all day. Its slogan was: 'Radio Caroline on 199 – your all-day music station'. Radio Luxembourg was also still providing an alternative to the BBC's pop output.

It was not until the turn of the decade that Radios 1 and 2 began to become independent of each other, and even then they were dogged by problems, especially Radio 2. The energy shortages of the 1970s were to play havoc with broadcasting: at times, Radio 2's early-morning shows were cancelled altogether, while presenters and time slots would be changed at a moment's notice, depending on whether broadcasting was actually going to be viable. It was a chaotic time – but Terry, as he had already proved over and again, was well equipped to deal with a little chaos.

His early training had served him very well, for Terry was by now something of a seasoned broadcaster, able to cope with almost anything that was flung his way. And, while he had been broadcasting on British radio for some time now, it was not until the end of the 1960s that he became a full-time presence on the new stations. And, with his strong Irish accent, he was a new kind of voice for the BBC.

Meanwhile, there was still a strong link between the two stations: David Hamilton's show was broadcast by both Radios 1 and 2 until, in 1977, he moved to Radio 2 alone. But, by the end of the 1970s, it was actually Radio 2 that was again breaking new ground: on 27 January 1979, it became the first British radio station to offer a 24-hour service. A new era in broadcasting had begun. By the time this came about, Terry had become as well known a face on television as he was a voice on the radio, but all that still lay ahead. For the present, he was concentrating on building up as big a following in Britain as he'd had in Ireland – something that did not take long to achieve.

It didn't take much time for the Wogans to realise that their gamble in moving to the UK was paying dividends. When Terry stood in for Jimmy Young in October 1969 it went so well that he was offered his own show: the original plan was to broadcast this on Radio 1, but, because of the lack of funding that affected so much else at the BBC at the time, it went out on both 1 and 2 between 3pm and 5pm. Terry's fan base widened and his celebrity, which had so far been confined mainly to Ireland, now began to grow in Britain.

Terry was revelling in it. At that time it was perhaps easier to be famous than it is now. The media was not so intrusive and, while boundaries across society were breaking down fast, there was still a hint of deference towards not only the great and the good but also the merely famous. Terry and Helen were able to lead a very agreeable lifestyle, mixing with their new friends and colleagues, while being relatively untroubled by the coverage Terry was now receiving. But, then again, there would have been nothing to worry about, even if the media had been as intrusive as they are nowadays. For Terry is one of those rare celebrities who has been an almost total stranger to scandal, marital or otherwise, and when it did touch him it came via a third person – one of his sons.

In the background, however, the shadow of the Troubles still hovered over the lustrous surface of Terry's new life. It would be putting it too strongly to say that the upheaval in Northern Ireland was at any time responsible for any real problems that confronted Terry, but it was an element in his life at that time. These days, his Irishness is just yet another reason for his popularity, but back then he sometimes worried that an Irish accent on British radio, following shortly after the news of an IRA attack, might provoke a backlash. His fears proved to be largely unfounded and, in fact, he was to find that any resentment towards him came as a response to his success, rather than to his nationality.

'It was a difficult time to be Irish, but I was in a privileged position and never experienced any prejudice in all that time,' he said in later years. 'I've had a couple of bomb threats and all that, but no one has ever been offensive towards me. I do know that all the time I was here it was tough on Irishmen in the streets, but I never felt we had anything to apologise for. I think obviously you will get people who begrudge you.

'As soon as you appear on the telly or the radio, there is going to be a high proportion of people who cannot stand the sight of you. You can't come on and exhibit any sort of personality and not expect people to be divided on you. The best you can hope for, if it is going to be successful, is 60 per cent in your favour and 40 per cent against you. It's human nature, you've got to accept that.'

As it happens, Terry easily got the 60 per cent (if not more) that he needed, mainly because it was fast becoming apparent what a strong personality the BBC had poached from the Emerald Isle. Terry's style of broadcasting might be genial, but it is also extremely topical, witty, sharp and occasionally barbed. Listening to his show wasn't, and still isn't, simply a cosy experience: back then, he was already quite capable of mocking humour, although he was certainly prepared to turn it on himself as much as on anyone else. He began to develop what is most important for an entertainer, a following. The very earliest incarnation of his fans, the 'TOGs', were tuning into his show in increasing numbers.

As his popularity continued to grow, the Wogan bandwagon quickly began to gather pace. In April 1972, Terry took over the breakfast show on Radio 2, where, with the exception of a television-inspired break in the 1980s, he has been ever since. The takeover was a sort of swap with John Dunn, who had been presenting the show and now moved to the afternoon slot for a while.

And it was that, more than anything else, that signalled what a success Terry was to become. The breakfast show has always been the most important for both Radios 1 and 2, because it gathers a huge listenership as people prepare for school and work, on top of which it sets the tone for the rest of the day. It is a very prestigious programme to present and it is awarded only to those who are considered the cream of the crop. There could be no better sign of the high esteem in which Terry was now held.

And it was now that the Wogan of today really began to emerge: Terry began to share his various obsessions with the listeners, who loved what they were hearing. They would write in to the station in their droves, which only increased the BBC's pleasure in its new find. The more the fans wrote, the more work Terry was offered, which meant he got more exposure, which in turn led to more letters. It was a virtuous circle that worked almost entirely to his benefit.

This was the beginning of an era of really serious success. Terry started winning awards hand over fist: he took the award for Radio Personality of the Year in 1974 and the Radio Award of the Radio Industries Club in 1974, 1976 and 1978. Invitations continued to flood in for television appearances, many of which he accepted. Terry was beginning to become a household name: his fame now extended far beyond the confines of Radio 2 as he was increasingly often recognised in the street. And, again, the better known he became, the more work he was offered. Nothing, as they say, succeeds like success.

Terry was certainly as famous in Britain now as he had been in Ireland, and, true to form, it was a state of affairs he handled with equanimity. Unlike so many people in show business, he rarely complains about the more intrusive aspects of being a celebrity, and he was also always at pains to avoid the excesses so often associated with being one. 'If you don't go out looking for trouble, it won't come and find you,' he said in later years. 'If you're Posh and Becks, you're going to get crucified. It has got much worse. It's no fun being well known any more. When I get offered a TV series now, I think, I don't want to do it because I don't want my name all over the papers.'

His home life remained a conventional one, and a happy one too. Terry and Helen settled into a large house on the Thames in Berkshire, where they have lived in some comfort ever since, and the family started to expand. The couple's second son, Mark, was born in 1970, followed by Katherine in 1972. The Wogans have always been absolutely scrupulous in not letting the death of their first daughter affect the way they treated their other children, but Terry has spoken since of the great joy he felt in having a second daughter. And it provided him with that all-important stability in the background that allowed him to take risks in the rest of his life and his career.

Because he had been making frequent television appearances, the more permanent move to TV didn't take long either, although it was to be a few more years before he ended up on the shows that were themselves to become household names. His first outing, in 1972, was *Lunchtime with Wogan,* a weekly show that went out on Tuesday on ATV and was meant to be ITV's riposte to the BBC's *Pebble Mill at One.*

His co-host was an Old English sheepdog, and while the show was not one of Terry's biggest successes – he once said it was ahead of its time – it did lead to a sketch called 'Christmas With Wogan' on ITV's *All Star Comedy Carnival* on Christmas Day that year. Just as he had done in radio, he was building up his confidence and gaining the experience that was to make him one of the most popular television presenters of all time.

Throughout it all, Terry kept his head. Modesty was always to the fore and angry outbursts were unheard of. The combination of his family and a good dose of common sense prevented him from throwing his weight around: the professionalism that is his hallmark was on show from the very start. This has also contributed to his longevity as a presenter: getting on and doing the work, without making a huge fuss about it, has always been Terry's style.

There was also more television work on the cards. This was the early 1970s, the days before beauty contests were all but banned from mainstream TV, and Terry found himself hosting the odd one of these. He also started to present *Come Dancing,* a programme that he was to stick with for the next seven years until, as he put it, he realised no one could ever remember who the presenter of the show was.

Despite his casual demeanour, Terry was prepared to work hard – but he did like to be appreciated for what he was doing. And he was absolutely right about the lack of recognition: *Come Dancing* had started in 1949 and since then it has had an enormous cast list of presenters who would go on to become famous, among them Michael Aspel, Judith Chalmers, Noel Edmonds and David Jacobs. Oddly enough, no one ever seems to remember them presenting the show, either.

Other programmes followed. In 1974, Terry undertook his first venture into the world of the chat show, a world that would reward him so well, when he hosted *Wogan's World.* Interviewees included Rolf Harris, Mary Quant and the astronomer Patrick Moore, and, while it didn't have the success *Wogan* would go on to have, it was good practice for what was to come. There were also increasing numbers of guest appearances on other television shows: among much else, Terry appeared on *Celebrity Squares,* which could be seen as some preparation for *Blankety Blank,* which it slightly resembled, and in an episode of *The Goodies* entitled 'Goodies Rule – O.K.?' He also started to present the odd *Eurovision Song Contest,* although it was to be a few more years before he made it his own.

And by now the Terry Wogan persona was firmly established. He was a generous man to work with, always allowing others their chance to shine, but at the same time he was clearly in charge of the proceedings – relaxed, confident and always up for a good joke. He had a ready wit, essential in a job like his, and the ability to keep his nerve, no matter how weird a situation became.

As to what it was that made him able to keep up the relentless banter, the jollity and the feat of being at one with the listener or viewer, Terry was as perplexed as anyone else. Asked in later years about his approach to being cheerful day after day, he replied, 'I put it down to clean living and the promise I made to my mother, many years ago, to keep myself pure and my bodily essences to myself. And also, that's what I do for a living! They pay me to do this. I know that's hard to believe.'

It certainly helped that Terry loved his work. Only a few years earlier he had been a bank clerk: now he was fast becoming a real star. He also took it more seriously than he would sometimes let on. It was still too soon to tell that this would be one of the truly great careers in broadcasting, but it was now clear that Terry had some quite exceptional qualities. If anyone was born to be a presenter, it was him. And he was about to have a major stroke of luck: he was going to be offered the opportunity to present one of the most popular game shows of all time.

His relentless cheeriness was becoming more popular by the day, but Terry still needed that major breakthrough and it was not until 1977 that it finally arrived. By now a well-established presence on the television, he was asked to present a new show on BBC1 called *Blankety Blank,* based on the US game show *The Match Game.* He himself would describe this as one of the most significant moments of his career: it was 'a watershed for me, the start of a decade of extraordinary success and acclaim'. It was also perfectly suited to his talents, as Terry later confirmed, admitting, 'I could make it up as I was going along.'

Since those days, *Blankety Blank* has received the kind of ire reserved for some of the worst television of all time, with *The Ultimate TV Guide,* for example, calling it a 'banal Saturday-evening game show'. But at the time the audience absolutely loved it, and they were a substantial proportion of the country. The premise was simple: Terry would give the contestants a phrase with one word blanked out. A panel of celebrities would write down that missing word and the contestant whose word matched that chosen by the most celebrities would be the winner of that round.

Terry presided as a master of ceremonies, keeping both the raucous celebrities and the nervous contestants under firm control. He had one prop: a deftly wielded tiny stick microphone, which became a comedy item in itself. The late DJ Kenny Everett, a man whose zaniness was more than a match for Terry's laidback drollery, would invariably sit bottom centre of the celebs, twisting his own microphone to comic effect. A typical panel would comprise Lorraine Chase, Frank Carson, Isla St Clair, Beryl Reid, Roy Kinnear and Bob Carolgees – a roll call of celebrities who were well known in the mid-1970s.

It was the kind of programme that needed someone who could think fast and was light on his feet. Given the amount of double entendre that the show almost inevitably involved, it also needed a squeaky-clean presenter, much in the same way that the show *Blind Date* needed a whiter-than-white presenter in the shape of Cilla Black. Terry Wogan was all of those things: he was gentle with the contestants and sharp, although never overly so, with the celebrities, and he managed to keep the proceedings in check whenever they threatened to get out of hand. Eventually to be given the crucial early-evening slot on Saturday night, *Blankety Blank* drew the kind of audiences television executives can only dream about now.

But still its success mystified many. '*Blankety Blank* is quite bonkers,' said an article in the *Radio Times* a couple of years after it began. 'The basic game is simple enough, but with all the accompanying fiddle-faddle – from the jangling signature jingle and Terry Wogan's preposterous microphone to those complications at the end – it's like some nightmare prank ... So why do 14 or 15 million perfectly sensible people sit mesmerised by it week after week?'

The answer was as simple as the programme's format – it made excellent telly. It allowed real people to appear on the screen (this was decades before reality TV, which sometimes seems to have paraded every individual in Britain across a television studio), and it had a panel of celebrities, seen as they were in real life as opposed to in the roles they played. It was even, once in a blue moon, an intellectual challenge, although, if truth be told, the audience was far more likely to tune in to hear Kenny Everett say something that was almost smutty than to listen out for the very rare occasion when real thoughtfulness was required.

Looking back on those far-off, innocent days, *Blankety Blank* seems to exist in a different era from the one that is reflected on television now. It was genuine family-friendly viewing: for all the naughty jokes, there was nothing you couldn't sit and watch with your dear old gran. There was no malice involved, no bitchery – apart from when the celebs sparred with each other – no mocking. It wasn't aimed at the nation's youth: it was aimed at everyone. And, childish as it might have appeared to some people, the show worked. A huge amount of that success was down to its host. Terry was relaxed, affable, charming and always in control. He never made a slip-up on screen, never allowed anyone to get the better of him. He was the perfect host for a brand-new (and slightly silly) game.

Naturally, the success of *Blankety Blank* increased Terry's stock with his employers. This was a time when competition between the BBC and ITV was reaching previously undreamed-of heights, with the ITV trying to poach as many of its rival's big names as it could get its hands on. And its approaches often worked. Perhaps the highest-profile defectors at the time were Morecambe and Wise, but commercial television was almost as keen to get its hands on Terry, and made him an offer to present a new show called *Game for a Laugh,* as *Blankety Blank'* s phenomenal popularity continued to grow. But, unlike so many others, Terry turned the offer down, judging, rightly as it turned out, that his 'prospects were better at the BBC'. Ultimately, Henry Kelly got the job on the new show, while Terry went on to earn still more plaudits at the BBC.

Despite his burgeoning television career, however, Terry's radio show was as important to him as ever. The nation adored his various obsessions and idiosyncrasies, which in turn led to plenty of memorable moments in his career, most notably when Terry had his one and only stint as a pop star, with a recording of the 'The Floral Dance' in 1978. It all began with Terry singing, during his show, over an instrumental hit by the Brighouse & Rastrick Brass Band about a traditional dance held at Helston, in Cornwall, once a year.

So popular did this become with the listeners that he was persuaded to record the number as a single in its own right, and so it was that Terry himself appeared on *Top of the Pops,* clad in bells and ribbons, singing and dancing away. It was quite as cringe-making as anything he would go on to present on the *Eurovision Song Contest,* but it was a modest hit nonetheless, reaching number 21 in the charts. Many years later, in 1995, it was recut and sold to benefit Children in Need. As for Terry, on the strength of all this excitement, 1978 was also the year he was asked to switch on the Blackpool Illuminations. It was an exciting time.

Another of his preoccupations was a campaign he termed 'Fight the Flab', a slot aimed at encouraging housewives to lose weight. This is now one of the most commonly used slogans in the whole of the huge dieting industry, but it was all Terry's own, something he is all too painfully aware of. 'Banjaxed is the word I brought to this island,' he once said. 'I also invented "fight the flab", which I should have copyrighted because people use it all the time now and I get no credit and, more importantly, no money.'

In inimitable Wogan style, he would mime pull-ups over the microphone and, as so often with Terry, there were various bizarre elements that all came together to maintain the whole. One of these came from Viv Stanshall of the Bonzo Dog Doo-Dah Band, who, for reasons too impenetrable to go into here, had been doing some work for the BBC.

'One of the problems doing Radio Flashes and other things for the Beeb was a continued battle with the establishment in order to gain access to the Radiophonic Workshop,' said the deeply eccentric Stanshall, sadly now dead, in an interview years ago. 'The Radiophonic Workshop is built like the bridge of a ship with so many knobs and twiddles. It's a nipple man's nightmare. You can get anything there. They've got white noise and pink noise and you start from there and what fun you could have. But you can't do that. What I wanted to do – do you remember Terry Wogan and his Fight the Flab? – I asked Terry Wogan if he'd do Fight the Flab if I provided flab.

'So what I wanted was to get an intelligent noise of flab so that Wogan would fight it in the ring while I did Kent Walton-style commentary from the outside. Terry Wogan broguely agreed. I tried it with balloons full of water and porridge and I couldn't get it right – I wanted flab bouncing off the ropes and hitting the canvas and he'd have a half-nelson on flab, who goes for a flying cross-buttock, etc. So it seemed that the only way I could do that would be to start with white noise. So I thought, Great, I'll go down to the Radiophonic Workshop, but you can't do that, you've got to write a specific script. And this was up through the Head of Department at Radio 1 and then to the Head of Department at Radio 3 or 4 and still you don't get into the room. It was clearly impossible. "Flab enters the room and removes his things: he postures and struts.'" One type of surrealism clearly attracted another.

The Fight the Flab slot became enormously popular. Terry would urge listeners to get up out of bed, swing their arms around and touch their toes to battle the bulge. One woman related that she was doing this stark naked when her husband unexpectedly returned home: a pregnancy subsequently ensued. In 1976, a seven-inch flexidisc entitled 'Fight the Flab with Terry Wogan' was given out free with Playtex girdles and bras. A book called *Fight the Flab: Keep Fit with Terry Wogan* also appeared. Like so much that Terry touched, the campaign was an uproarious success.

Terry's greatest and most successful obsession – if an obsession can be regarded as a success – came a few years later. It began when a new television show, an American import, started on the BBC. The show was quite unlike anything anyone had ever seen before: set among the super-rich of Texas, it had a cast of characters whose wealth was matched only by their mendacity and whose lives seemed to consist of one devious scheme after another. It was, of course, *Dallas,* home to the inimitable Ewing family, and it almost immediately became a nationwide obsession in Britain.

No one was more fascinated by *Dallas* than Terry and it fast became one of the most popular subjects on his show. He talked about it endlessly, until the Terry take on *Dallas* became almost as popular as the television series itself. Some people think that the two were strongly connected. 'Rightly or wrongly, I was perceived in the BBC as the main architect in the runaway success of *Dallas* with the British viewing public,' Terry later recalled.

'The rumour had started on my Radio 2 morning programme, with a few observations from me concerning the apparent fact that, although richer than Croesus, the Ewing family of Dallas had only one telephone – in the hall; that they had walk-in wardrobes, but only wire coat hangers ... The listeners, bless 'em, responded; *Dallas* became a cult and then a full-blown ratings winner. It was like a weekly *Eurovision Song Contest.*

'Over the top, full of ridiculous characters, deeply, deeply foolish and riveting to watch. Americans watched *Dallas* from an entirely different viewpoint than we did. They thought it was a drama of everyday Texan oil billionaires; we thought it was a comedy. We were right.'

The Americans caught on eventually, though – witness this remark from Jock, the paterfamilias: 'Bobby has the capacity to forgive and forget. That's a shame. A damn shame.'

Terry would pick up on anything and everything that caught his eye where the Ewings were concerned. Another running joke was JR's skin colour: because the quality of the picture was not as good as it was in the US, Terry would comment that you never knew what strange colour of green Larry Hagman, who played the enormously popular character, would appear to be from one week to the next. It was Terry who dubbed Lucy Ewing 'the poison dwarf', and he would even write articles about the subject, on one occasion voicing concern that, although the characters regularly appeared in front of plates positively groaning with food, they never actually got to eat any of it.

'My heart goes out to old Jock Ewing,' he wrote, 'every time I see him about to sink the bicuspids into the lightly grilled back-rasher, only to find the forkful frozen halfway to its destination by Pammy storming from the room in a marked manner or Sue-Ellen storming into it the worse either for drink, JR, Cliff Barnes, the steely-haired psychiatrist...' There was a good deal more in this vein, each piece more amusing than the last and proof of another of Terry's talents – he's a very good writer too.

Terry's fascination with *Dallas* led to a television programme that was so successful that it has been repeated several times since: an interview with Larry Hagman himself. It was serendipity: all the elements came together at once. *Dallas* fever was at its height: it was a few years into the programme and the makers of the show had engineered one of the most successful cliffhangers in television history. The whole world seemed to be obsessed with who shot JR, the calculating, amoral, malevolent and utterly compelling scion of the Ewing dynasty, and it was a question that was to dominate the media for months to come.

With this question still hanging in the air, Hagman himself decided it was an ideal time to visit the UK, and it was a visit that could not have been better timed for all concerned.

Hagman – like the producers of *Dallas* themselves – was at that time not sure whether JR was to survive: if he did, this was an ideal time to renegotiate his contract. So he decided to make himself scarce for a while, reasoning that absence makes the heart grow fonder and, in this case, the pocket deeper.

It is impossible to tell if Hagman realised at that point quite how hugely popular he and the show were around the rest of the world, but his strategy was quite brilliant: it kept him constantly in the headlines, and the audience clamouring for more. In addition, it provided Terry with one of the most memorable hours of television that 1980 produced.

Hagman himself certainly didn't fully realise exactly what lay in store, although he was utterly thrilled by the reaction his presence provoked. 'What I did was take a trip to London just before the JR shooting episode hit the air in March,' Larry later recalled. 'This was partly for fun and partly because it is a good idea to put 6,000 or so miles between you and your employers in a situation like this. It's surprising what a soothing effect geography can have at times. They get very edgy when they can't find you right away. My wife and I got off the plane at Heathrow to be greeted by a yelling, screaming, pushing, shoving mob

of photographers, shooting through their legs, if necessary, to get the picture.

'Next day, I went on television, jet lag and all, with an inventive Irish disc jockey named Terry Wogan, who ordinarily appeared on radio, [but] had made himself the talk of Britain with a running take-off of *Dallas.* It had built to a point where the BBC had offered him an hour-long special if I would do it with him. The British love anything Texan anyway, and we had a field day. The ratings were the highest of the year. I had taken a ten-gallon hat with me. In that cowboy-crazy place, it offered unmistakable and immediate identification. It became my trademark from then on. I might never have left London if I hadn't contracted to do the film *S.O.B.* for Blake Edwards.'

Terry also adored the whole experience. 'A television producer named Frances Whittaker got the bright idea of bringing over Larry and having a TV confrontation: JR meets TW,' he said. 'It was my first-ever television talk show [*sic*] and I loved it. I could not have had a better guest than Hagman – he played the JR role to the hilt, slipping in and out of character like the terrific pro he is.' And little did Terry realise it, but this encounter was to prove highly significant for him in his own career: it had illustrated to his bosses at the BBC just how good he was at making famous guests relax and chat. Of course, the guests had to be right, as Hagman had been, but there was clearly the germ of an idea here as to what Terry was capable of, given the chance to plunge into new challenges. The seed did not take long to grow.

And the BBC loved him. It also permitted Terry a special licence for mockery: he played the court jester in the land where the Director-General was king. On his radio show, Terry has always mocked the powers that be, none more so than Ian Trethowan, who was DG of the BBC between 1977 and 1982. 'I defy anyone to sit in the chair of the Director-General and not be moved by a sense of history,' Trethowan declared. 'Even the cheerfully mischievous inventions of Terry Wogan underline how important a position it is.'

And Terry indeed gave the Director-General a special place on the radio show, repeatedly sighting him 'just putting in his dentures'. He was forever seeing him, as the DG himself put it, in 'extremely undignified and risible situations. It seemed to me that Terry's joking helped in a small way to humanise an office which must otherwise seem very remote to ordinary listeners.' A bridge between the famous and important and the man in the street is a role Terry has played ever since.

Terry had now proven himself to be one of the most versatile performers the country had ever seen. He was equally comfortable in television and radio, moving with ease between the two, and he had shown he could turn his hand to presenting almost anything. He could front chat shows, the *Eurovision Song*

Contest and *Blankety Blank,* and all of that without letting it go to his head. The great skill in acting, they say, is to make it look easy, and this is what Terry was doing with everything he touched: he made it look so simple that no one could have guessed that what he was doing was actually a highly skilled job.

Yet, behind it all ran that stream of self-deprecation. Asked recently why he was famous, Terry replied, 'I am famous – because good looks have to count for something,' before going on to talk about the fact that he'd been very lucky. He had, but there was a good deal of talent there too. There was also a readiness to work hard.

There had been that early commuting between England and Ireland, and now there was a huge amount of radio and television work, which, although enjoyable, was again very wearing. Few presenters have ever had a workload anything like as heavy as Terry's, but he was determined to continue doing as much as he was able to fit in.

And now, at the start of the 1980s, he was ready to take on the programme that was going to make him more famous still. Terry's career was going from strength to strength: he was wildly popular among radio listeners and television viewers, and by this time pretty much had his pick of anything the BBC wanted to offer. And it had quite an offer up its sleeve, which led to Terry, a middle-class boy from average beginnings in Limerick, becoming one of the most famous people in the country.

5

THRICE-WEEKLY WOGAN

Every successful career is built on two essentials: talent and luck. You can have as much of the first as you like, but without the second you will never get anywhere, and nowhere is this more the case than in show business. The world of the performing arts is about as insecure a field as any that exists and Terry himself has always acknowledged how fortunate he has been. Timing is all and cannot be bettered as a strategy, and it was because of this combination of talent, luck and timing that Terry found himself where he was in the early 1980s.

'I am famous because I am lucky and everyone who is famous ought to remember that,' he said. 'Sometimes people who are tremendously famous imagine it is due to their own brilliance. It is partly due to whatever tiny talent they have but you have to be lucky and you have to be in the right place at the right time. And what you have to offer has to be relevant to whatever you are being offered. Then you might be successful.'

That is as accurate a summary of Terry's career as any could be. Not only has he managed repeatedly to be in the right place at the right time, but also his particular brand of broadcasting has proven to be perfectly suited to the times. From the controlled zaniness of *Blankety Blank* to his affable mastery of the chat show, Terry has managed to provide exactly what the audiences want to see and hear. And then there is his ability to chime with the country's preoccupations, as he did to such enormous effect with his fascination with *Dallas.* He connects with his audience and speaks as they want to be spoken to. It is a talent that few other broadcasters possess.

His utter professionalism has also meant that there was never any hint of ructions behind the scenes, especially where his family was concerned. Terry's marriage to Helen might have been as solid as a rock, but there was the odd problem involving his children, of which more later on. This was never allowed to show. Terry might harp on about his personal obsessions on air, but he gives remarkably little of himself away – something that is very rarely realised. Just as when he was a child, he still liked to go home and shut the door on the world. Nor did he socialise too much in the glitzier realms of the showbiz world. His favourite place was still at home with Helen.

And Terry has been famous for so long now it is sometimes easy to forget that not everything he touched turned to gold. There were quite a few deferred successes along the way, as everyone sought a piece of Terry and he himself looked for the right vehicle to best use his talents. Sometimes everyone got it wrong, and one such programme was called *You Must Be Joking.*

This was 'a comedy game show about hoaxes, spoofs, put-ons and tall stories', according to the *Radio Times.* 'Each week two teams of contestants, as well as all the family at home, will find out just how gullible they really are by judging the authenticity of obscure objects, fractured facts, faulty films and the surprising secrets of a Star Personality.' Described by one critic as 'an attempt to justify Terry Wogan's salary of x,000 licence fees', it didn't last long.

It didn't really matter: Terry was on a roll. He still had *Blankety Blank,* for which the public appetite showed no sign at all of abating, and he was about to embark on a programme that was to become more successful still. And, in a roundabout way, this new opportunity presented itself because of one of the other grandees of BBC broadcasting: Michael Parkinson. 'Parky' had spent years hosting one of the most successful television chat shows of all time, but in the early 1980s he caused shock waves across the Corporation when he defected to TV-am.

The competition between all the channels, including those that were newly created, was as intense as ever: each was looking to pick famous scalps from the opposition and the bigger the name the bigger the embarrassment and upset it caused to its rivals. And Parkinson's departure left a huge gap in the BBC schedule and precipitated an immediate race to find a candidate to step into his not inconsiderable boots.

Terry was quite clearly the man for the job. He had already been fronting a chat show with the late Paula Yates, which had been very well received, while his interview with Larry Hagman had been widely acknowledged as an enormous success. He was the obvious candidate for the vacancy created by Parkinson. There was intense speculation in the press about who should adopt the seasoned interviewer's mantle and the smart money was on Terry – indeed, there really was no other candidate on the cards for the job. It was the type of broadcasting at which he excelled: a show with a relaxed format, spilling over with bonhomie, in which his personality came to the fore while at the same time still allowing the guests to shine. As a result, it was not long before he was confirmed as the man for the job.

Terry was not, however, going to be Parkinson-lite. 'My show will be different from Parkinson's because I am different from Parkinson,' he said in 1983. 'Parkinson interviews. What I want is conversation. He is a journalist by training. I've no journalistic training. I shall act more as a catalyst and not give my guest a hard ride. I'd like to get them away from their routine. If you let them, they'll give you their chat-show routine which they've done for everyone else.' This proved to be an excellent strategy: for many years, *Wogan* was unquestionably the most prestigious chat show on television.

The programme began to air in January 1983, with Terry an enormously popular choice for the slot. 'It's hard to believe now, after the contumely and abuse of the latter days of *Wogan* in the Nineties, but the press were all for me then,' Terry said years later. '"Give him his own chat show with all the old Parkinson trimmings, and just watch the redoubtable Terry take off!"' And take off he did: *Wogan,* which at first went out on Saturday nights, was a triumph from the start.

Although the show would almost certainly have worked as a result of Terry's presence alone, the quality of the guests almost certainly helped. An early one was Cilla Black, whose appearance was such a triumph that it led to a revival of her own career. 'Cilla Black had been in the shadows for some time when she came on *Wogan* and awoke the nation anew to her talents with a hilarious routine about a Liverpool radio phone-in show,' Terry later recalled. 'On the other side of the Thames, Alan Boyd [at LWT] spotted her.' Cilla, like Terry a few years before, had been looking for a television show that was ideally suited for her talents and would allow her to step back into the limelight: shortly after appearing on *Wogan,* she found just such a vehicle in the shape of *Blind Date.*

Among Terry's other guests was another *Dallas* star, Victoria Principal, who had played Pammy – Terry ended up admitting that he had not actually read the book she had come on the show to talk about, which only increased the programme's appeal – and the comedian Freddie Starr, who, Terry later revealed, had required some delicate editing. He described Starr as the world's most frightening interviewee. By the end of the run, in April that year, Terry's new position as a chat-show king was secure. He was, as he said, not a new version of Parkinson, but indisputably an interviewer with his own style, a star in his own right.

The programme, and Terry's way of fronting it, worked for many reasons. His approach was very much one of bonhomie: rather than ask his guests too many embarrassing questions, he would treat them as if they were an old friend who had dropped in for a chat. This had the effect of making the audience feel exactly the same way about the famous stars appearing on screen, and at its best the show almost made the viewers believe they were watching someone they knew. This had its downside, though, for when it went badly, as it occasionally did, it was not easy to rescue the situation. Nonetheless, the general feeling of bonhomie was exactly what the audience wanted right from the start.

The new show was on its way. But with that workload – Terry was still doing his morning radio show and making a great number of additional television appearances, as well as fronting two prime-time shows – something had to give and that something turned out to be *Blankety Blank.* The show had been an exceptional success: it had ended up being moved to the prestigious Saturday-night slot and at its peak in 1979 had attracted an extraordinary 23.3 million viewers. But, in 1984, because of his other work commitments, Terry decided that he and *Blankety Blank* would finally go their separate ways, although the union had been an extremely happy one.

'From the start I loved it,' said Terry. 'At last, I was not trapped in a tuxedo or behind a desk. The ridiculous microphone gave me something to do with at least one hand. I could walk and talk where I liked, without looking for marks on the floor. *Blankety Blank* was the first time I felt as easy in front of a TV camera as I always had before a radio mike.' It had certainly made an impact. Although it is now more than 20 years since Terry left the show, there is still a substantial proportion of the population who can remember him, silly mike and all, asking celebrity guests to fill in the blankety blank.

It was a wise decision, though. Only once has Terry's sense of timing deserted him, and that was nearly a decade later, when *Wogan,* which by this time was being shown during the week rather than on Saturday nights, finally came to a belated end. As it was, not only had he been fronting *Blankety Blank* for years now and so risked going stale – although that never actually happened – but also he was doing so much else that he was opening himself to the charge of overexposure, which is again what happened ten years on. The wisest maxim in show business (and life) is 'Always leave them wanting something more', and so Terry wisely bowed out before anyone else actually wanted him to leave the stage. It seemed that an era in television history had come to an end.

But, although its star was leaving, the powers that be took the decision that the show must go on. It might not have had the audience that it did at the end of the 1970s, but it was still pulling in around 11 million viewers – a massive number by today's standards – and it was felt there was life in the old format yet. But who was to take on Terry's role? In the event, much to the surprise of the public, it turned out to be the late great comedian Les Dawson, whose persona – dour, Northern and grumpy – was a world away from Terry's relaxed Irish charm. Yet it was a good choice, for a presenter with a style too like Terry's would have merely appeared as a paler version of him, whereas Les Dawson was so different that ultimately he was judged for himself, rather than the man he was replacing.

Dawson, one of the most popular comedians of the 20th century, came from a very different background from Terry. He learned his trade on the Northern standup circuit, which made him as able as Terry to deal with any vicissitudes that came his way. A formidable presence – and, like Terry, a highly likeable man – Les was famous for the accents he put on, the faces he could pull. Sadly no longer with us, Les was one of the comedy giants and is fondly remembered to this day.

Even so, it was a daunting task that he was taking on. 'It's not an easy show to do,' Les said. 'And Terry is a hard man to follow. He had his own style and it would be a waste of time trying to be a clone and copy him. You have to put your own stamp on whatever you do and find your own style.' It was a brave move to assume Terry's mantle. Even Les's wife, Meg, was wary about his taking on a role that Terry seemed to have made his own, and it took a good month before the critics conceded that they had a worthy successor to Mr Wogan on their hands. But Les, taking on board Meg's concerns, did some careful preparation behind the scenes before finally deciding to go ahead, which he did partly because, just like Terry, he was prepared to take risks.

'I was a little doubtful when it was first suggested and that is why I insisted on doing two pilots that never went out before making a final decision,' he said. 'I wanted to make sure it wasn't going to be disastrous. I believe you have got to take chances in this business if you want to progress. It is true that I have been very successful as a stand-up comic, but I feel you need to change what you are doing now and again.

'*Blankety Blank* seemed a great opportunity to do something different, although there were obvious pitfalls. The main one was that, however good I was, I would be compared unfavourably with Terry. But I decided to go ahead and do it my way. There would have been no point in setting out to be a clone. And

I stuck by that even when things weren't going well. It was the old thing of being true unto yourself. I always try to ignore the critics and leave the public to make their own minds up.'

Eventually, of course, critics and public alike were completely won over and, ironically, after Dawson's death in 1993, four years after the show had finally gone off air, Terry was approached by the BBC to host a new series. He refused, not least because it would have been a step backwards in career terms and he had new projects to think about. But critics also noted that, had he done it, now he would be judged against Les, rather than the other way around!

Even without *Blankety Blank,* Terry still had a very full agenda, though, given that he continued to appear frequently on other television shows and at that point still had his radio programme, and he acknowledged this fact years later. 'I have an easy life,' he said, once he had calmed his schedule down. 'I have always had an easy life. I used to work very hard one time. Come in to do a morning radio show, then open a Tesco store in Dorset or someplace and then come back and do *Come Dancing.*

'But it never seemed like work, although opening supermarkets and personal appearances can be hard work. I remember standing on a table in Portsmouth once and the crowd crashed in through the plate-glass window. The manager got really annoyed and said it would be the last time he'd have me there. He got the crowd, but he didn't like the way they were ruining his store.' Terry, however, never let himself be fazed by these events. Always the consummate professional, he continued to have the public eating out of his hand.

For this was the period when Terry's popularity seemed to soar with every day that passed. His face and his voice were everywhere. He seemed to win every award going, for his work on both radio and television. He was a proven wit and raconteur. Sometimes it seemed that a week without Terry somewhere on the television was a rare week indeed. And the public appetite for him did not seem possible to sate: people adored him and, when they were given more of him, they wanted still more.

Wogan started its second run with Terry continuing to be as genial as ever. Guests queued to come on: Terry's affability made many of them so relaxed that they appeared at their best – and the stars liked that. Of course, the public did too. The show was such a success that the BBC's formatters now began thinking of something quite radical at the time: expanding it to several nights a week – and, with hindsight, perhaps this was not quite the right decision to make for the longer term. A lot of a good thing can become too much and it risked spreading Terry too thinly.

But it was a new idea that appealed to everyone at the time, and so it was agreed that *Wogan* would be moved from the weekend and put on during the week instead. There was initially some talk of Terry doing a nightly late-night talk show, of the kind already popular on American television, but eventually, in 1985, it was decided that it should go out three times a week in an early-evening slot. This decision actually took quite some time to come to.

Bill Cotton, the BBC's Managing Director of Television Services, was fresh from the success of introducing *EastEnders* – then must-see television, although it certainly isn't now – the year before, and was keen to see Terry make the move. 'Originally my idea had been that Terry should do a late-night show along the lines of the one hosted by Johnny Carson in the United States, but Terry preferred an earlier slot, which had more chance of attracting his large Radio 2 morning-programme audience,' he said.

This doesn't quite fit in with how everyone remembered it: Terry knew that, if he took the new job, he would have to leave his radio show, partly because the workload would have exhausted him and partly because, even for a presenter as popular as he was, starting the day with hours of him on the radio and ending it with hours of him on television would have been a bit too much. More likely was that Terry, who has never made any secret of his fondness for food nor of his wife's prowess in the kitchen, wanted to be able to get home to have dinner with Helen every night.

And Michael Grade, then Controller of BBC1, said there were other reasons for choosing the early-evening slot. There was only a certain amount of leeway in the evening's schedules and, given that this was to be a programme that went out frequently, it couldn't be allowed to cause too much disruption to what else was on the box. Indeed, Grade gave a revealing insight into how television schedules are put together and how even exceptionally popular presenters like Terry must still fit in with the overall mix of what a channel puts out.

'Bill Cotton was keen to use Terry three nights a week at the end of the evening,' he said. 'I just didn't see how I could carve out the necessary space because I was constrained by the position of the *Nine O'Clock News,* which was immovable. The programme that followed it was the main entertainment of the late evening and might be a drama, a film, a comedy or an American show. All these programmes were of different lengths, so I couldn't offer a fixed starting time for *Wogan* at the end of the evening. I was also worried that many of Terry's natural viewers would be in bed by the time we screened it late at night – I therefore decided to put out *Wogan* at seven o'clock on Mondays, Wednesdays and Fridays.'

And then there was Terry himself to consider, not merely in terms of the time the show would go out but whether he wanted to do it at all. This was a very big move. He was firmly established on both radio and television, but this show was a largely untested format: if the idea failed, it would be – because of Terry's involvement – a very high-profile failure, and one that would be laid at his door. And then there was the radio programme: he was clearly going to have to give that up too. In the event, he thought the gamble was worth it, but it was not a decision taken lightly.

'A thrice-weekly show would mean me giving up the daily radio show and, of course, the Saturday-night chat show,' he later recalled. 'It was a big decision. I could sit tight on the success of both these shows, and go on forever, or as long as anybody goes on in this strange game. I did not have to take the risk; I was sitting pretty on top of the ratings and the popularity polls.' But, as before, he decided in the end to take the risk, and so it was that he found himself in one of the defining jobs of his career.

Wogan, or rather the thrice-weekly *Wogan,* was a minisensation. Nothing like this had ever been done before. His early-morning radio show may now be the most popular programme on radio, but it is fair to say that for a while, at least, something similar could have been said of his television talk show: it played a hugely important part in the nation's viewing throughout the late 1980s and early 1990s and it is for that, as well as his radio work, that Terry will be best remembered.

And for all the politicking that went on about the show's eventual timeslot, to say nothing of accommodating Terry's dining preferences, it is fair to say that its early-evening position led to Terry taking one step further into the nation's consciousness. It is often said that people who, via television, appear regularly in the nation's living rooms seem to become part of each individual family watching, and nowhere was this more the case than with Terry Wogan. The show went out at a time when it could be watched by children who had finished their homework, by whole families either during or after the evening meal and even by people who had other plans for the evening but who had the television on in the background as they prepared to go out.

A massive amount of attention was given by the press to this scheduling. Not only was this the first time anyone had put a talk show on three times a week, but also Terry had been heavily lobbied for in the media. He was the people's presenter, as it were: the newspapers wanted him because their readers did, and so they were only too happy to act as cheerleaders once the show was clearly about to go ahead. There can rarely have been another occasion on which a show was launched with so much sheer goodwill: everyone was willing it to succeed from the start.

The timing of the show meant that content had to be carefully monitored – there was no chance of any outrage on *Wogan,* apart from the odd unscripted crisis, but when that happened, as with George Best's appearance, of which more below, the nation seemed to sympathise with Terry as he coped with a difficult guest. It was as if Terry was a much-loved uncle, chatting away to his celebrity friends and introducing them to all the family. A late-night show would have had a totally different feel and, very likely, nothing like the same mass appeal. It was yet another example not only of Terry being in the right place at the right time but also of his having exactly the right talents for what was to remain an incredibly popular show for years.

The thrice-weekly *Wogan* was to run for seven years in total and, like its Saturday-night predecessor, was an immediate success. And it really did attract all the big names, with the first show numbering Elton John among its guests. Such was Terry's excitement that he tripped up and fell over, Elton helped him up and the audience roared their applause. It certainly did nothing to hurt the programme's pulling power: Paul McCartney appeared on it five times, Peter Cushing four times and Kenneth Williams an astonishing 11 times, although that did include three stints as a guest presenter, which in turn became yet more memorable episodes in themselves.

Early interviewees included Dolly Parton, Don Johnson (via satellite) and Mel Brooks, although names such as these were just a hint of what was to come: vast numbers of the great, the good and the infamous would appear on *Wogan* over the years. And Terry's style, relaxed and informal as ever, was also new to the small screen. Terry became famous for doing as little research on the people who appeared on his show as he could get away with, which in many cases meant just about no research at all. 'I'm a great believer in spontaneity, mainly because I don't have the capacity to take pains,' he said. Again, he made it look easy, which it wasn't – it was simply a way of presenting that was entirely in tune with Terry's persona.

He had clearly come into his own. By this point, Terry was a very experienced television presenter: he had been broadcasting for over 20 years and his experience showed. If his guests were nervous, he could usually bring them out of themselves; if they were too exuberant, he calmed them. He was also adept at switching the topic of conversation when it got too close to the bone. On one occasion, Kenneth Williams began to air some fairly eye-watering views about the death penalty, but Terry gently headed him off and got on to safer ground.

And then there were the guests. Alongside the truly stellar names, Kenneth Williams, when kept away from contentious subjects, was far and away one of the most entertaining guests on the show, with a wealth of anecdotes, some new, some on their second or third outing. As he recalled it, 'I did the Orson on vowels, Guinness on flies and Siobhan and the bishop and Edith Evans and basting.' On another occasion, he, Terry, David Jason and Julie Walters took part in a live party on New Year's Eve 1985 in front of, as he put it, 'a bemused audience dressed in paper hats', while on a separate outing he appeared to be chatting in front of a whelk stall. The chemistry between Kenneth and Terry was perfect: Terry's charm softened the Williams acerbity. They made a very good match.

Right from the start, Terry was not especially proprietorial about the show: he was perfectly happy to let guest presenters take the chair. Ultimately, some of them went on to host shows in their own right. Kenneth Williams's first stint in the inquisitor's chair came about in 1986 and there was initially some concern that his own verbosity would prove too much for the guests to cope with: in the event, however, the producers solved this problem by littering the show with his friends, including Barbara Windsor, Derek Nimmo and Nicholas Parsons.

Ultimately, it proved to be a great success. Highlights of the week included a limerick competition, and Kenneth finished on a high note, singing, to the tune of 'My Bonnie', 'Bring back, bring back, bring back Terry Wogan to me, to me, bring back Terry Wogan to me!' Unsurprisingly, it brought the house down. Rather sadly, Kenneth's last-ever television appearance was on Terry Wogan's show, not long before his death in 1988.

Never mind the guests – *Wogan* even attracted a high calibre of guest hosts when Terry was away. Apart from Kenneth Williams, these included Sue Lawley, Selina Scott, Joanna Lumley, Clive Anderson, Bruce Forsyth, Gloria Hunniford and Ronnie Corbett.

Meanwhile, anyone who was anyone in show business in the late 1980s seemed to be a guest on the show at one time or another.

Nor was it Williams alone who made the programme momentarily his. Another much talked-about interview took place when Sue Lawley was hosting *Wogan.* Her guest that night was the fashion designer Vivienne Westwood. Westwood's designs, based on medical clothing, were paraded in front of an audience that promptly fell to pieces laughing: Vivienne became so annoyed that she told Sue that, if the audience didn't stop its hilarity, she would stop the models from coming out.

The show fast established itself as a worthy rival to the mighty *Parkinson.* It is generally agreed that Wogan is really the only real rival Parky ever had when it came to establishing who had presented the really truly great British chat show. In later years, Terry came in for a great deal of criticism about the supposedly self-satisfied air resting like a blanket over the show, but, to begin with, it was an enormous and deserved success.

Terry somehow seemed to bridge the gap between celebrity and the everyday: although hugely successful in his own right, he somehow seemed to empathise with the viewer at home as much as the celebrity on the sofa. Terry has never been unwise enough to think himself above the man in the street: on television, as much as the radio, that has a great deal to do with his success.

However, it was not unknown for Terry to feel unsympathetic towards his guests – although this never came across on the screen – for example when his guest was David Bowie, who failed to co-operate with the interview. A quite different side of Terry came to light then: one which was utterly professional, utterly dedicated to making the programme work and utterly disgusted with anyone who seemed willing to put a spanner in the works. Nor was he afraid to speak his mind. 'He [Bowie] would not speak, or at least, not sensibly,' Terry snarled later. 'He will never know how close he came to a slap on live television.' It would certainly have got the viewers talking.

On another occasion, he was asked which of his guests he had wanted to throttle the most. The answer appeared to be an awful lot of them. 'HRH Prince Philip, John Malkovich, Vanessa Redgrave, Anne Bancroft, Stewart Granger and Spike Milligan,' he said. 'Prince Philip is a boring old ... He came on and he wanted to talk about carriage driving. He didn't understand why no one was interested. I think it was in that interview that he said he didn't understand why more people didn't play polo. And Spike Milligan was always difficult. He was a good friend of mine and, as any of his friends will tell you, Spike could come and go. He was a manic-depressive. If you got him when he was manic, he would drive you mad. I think I preferred him when he was depressed.'

Anne Bancroft really had riled him. The problem was that she had not realised the show went out live and came to Terry in tears in his dressing room when she found that that was the case. Her nerves showed through: she was forced to count to ten at the top of the staircase leading to the set and even then was so terrified she was only able to answer his questions in monosyllables. It was something Terry returned to more than once in the future.

'I don't know,' he replied when asked who had been the worst guest on his show. 'Anne Bancroft was no picnic. She wouldn't speak. But there were a lot of what I would call eejits. American actors who thought you should be plugging their film or book as soon as they came out. Bette Davis was difficult. John Malkovich was no picnic.' Nor was Chevy Chase, who remained largely silent throughout his interview, but it was Anne Bancroft whose behaviour stayed with him till the last. And he was never allowed to forget it: when the actress died in the summer of 2005, Terry revealed that even then, nearly two decades later, people still reminded him of that show in all its crushing awfulness.

Given the longevity of the show, and the fact that it was on three times a week, it is not surprising that some moments remain in the public consciousness to this day. One memorable occasion took place in 1990 when a drunk George Best lurched on to the set: Best's problems with alcohol were not as widely known about then as they are now, and his appearance on the show caused something of a sensation. He started swearing and slurring, prompting Terry to cut short the interview, which was going out live.

The country was outraged that Best had been allowed to appear in such a condition and there were even suggestions that the producers of the show had encouraged him to have too much to drink before he came on – something that was strenuously denied by all involved. Terry was particularly irritated by the charge. 'I love George Best and I never thought he was a bad guest,' he said. 'When I left him, he was perfectly sober. He must have drunk very quickly between the time I left the hospitality box and the time he came on the set, because he was out of his mind.'

Best himself realised it had not been his finest hour. 'The worst thing was that I thought I'd got away with it, that, although I might have been a bit tipsy, I had come across as reasonably coherent,' he wrote afterwards. 'But, when I saw the recording the following day, it was obvious I had been completely out of it ... it's awful to see yourself coming across as some mumbling drunk.'

On another occasion, David Icke, a young footballer turned television presenter turned Green Party spokesman, appeared: he caused national consternation when he announced that he was a 'son of the Godhead'. The audience watched open-mouthed as Icke, dressed in a turquoise shell suit, gave increasingly strange answers, until Terry, in a rare moment when he showed that inner steel, leaned forward and said, 'They're not laughing with you, David. They're laughing at you.'

And then there were the guests who had quite clearly taken drugs. Terry was not impressed: for a start, it was totally unprofessional and, secondly, it made for problems on the show. 'I used to get furious inside,' Terry said. 'I'm not a great fan of anybody, so I'd be looking at them ... You get a bloody actor who's on an upper or a downer – too far over the top because he's taken something up his nose or another pill – and you think, Why come on the show if you don't want to talk? Idiot.'

Terry himself found that his favourite guests were not actually the famous ones. 'It was the human-interest ones, the Simon Westons, that interested me most,' he said. 'Showbiz is just showbiz.' Nor did he spend huge amounts of time schmoozing with the celebrities he met: he later said that his favourite part of the day came later, when he was back at home having dinner with Helen.

'That was the high spot,' he said comfortably. 'I used to go up to "Hostility", have a drink with the eejits, then go home and have my dinner and never have to watch it. I never watch myself.' It was a wise strategy. On another occasion, he talked again about the dangers of watching yourself and inadvertently developing a hugely irritating trademark tic – like Anne Robinson being trapped behind her wink.

And still he kept his feet on the ground. Terry himself believed that one of the reasons the show – and, indeed, the other television he did – worked so well was that he had the right attitude towards it. 'I have never thought what I do is terribly important,' he said. 'I deliberately don't allow myself to get worked up as nerves don't serve you on radio and television. Nerves help when you are on the stage when you are in the theatre. But on television the viewers can see straight into your eyes and know this man is terrified. That embarrasses them, so they switch you off.'

That was certainly one factor in the show's success: his ability to relax. If he ever felt nerves, he never showed them. Even in the middle of the George Best fiasco, Terry didn't panic: he took control of the situation and ushered his guest out of sight. Long, long gone was the nervous young broadcaster who could hardly get through his first show on air: in his place was a massively experienced and professional presenter who could cope with just about anything. Terry was lively but never frenetic. It made for a perfect image and the viewers lapped it up.

To this day, *Wogan* in its heyday remains unmatched. It takes a phenomenal talent to appear fresh night after night, to cope with the unexpected and simply to exist under all the public scrutiny directed your way. Terry has always led a very unstarry existence, and his personal life, given that he married young and is still married to the same woman, has never given rise to any controversy. Yet it is not easy to live under the constant glare of the spotlight and, when the show finally began to fall from favour, Terry had to put up with a good deal of public ribbing – and sometimes worse.

With hindsight, it is possible to see that the little niggles that eventually became so overwhelming were right there from the start. It was by no means only in the later years of *Wogan* that the press was sometimes unkind: there were sour mutterings from some corners shortly after the show began, and Terry acknowledged this in 1986, when he won the award for Favourite Male TV Personality at the TV Times Top Ten Awards, for the eighth year running. His acceptance speech betrayed a certain amount of discontent.

'I don't get blasé, because they are the only television awards that mean anything, as they are made by the public itself,' he said. 'The fact that *Wogan* is on BBC and *TV Times* viewers have voted for me means that those who watch television are not bothered by the barriers. I've found this reward quite gratifying this year because, over the last few months, I've been the target of a fair amount of abuse in print.' It was, alas, a harbinger of what was to come.

For Terry was to make a very rare misjudgement over *Wogan:* he simply allowed it to go on for too long.

Because the show was on so often in the early evening, he himself had almost become part of the wallpaper: he was, simply, always there. People had got so used to seeing him that they no longer appreciated him: what had started out as charming, Irish wit now seemed too complacent and self-satisfied to produce really compelling television. Familiarity had bred contempt. Perhaps if the show had been on late at night and therefore prone to occasional moments of outrage, it might have lasted longer, but more likely is the conclusion that it simply ran its course.

The end, when it came, was not particularly easy for anyone involved. Other areas of the media, namely newspapers, were not actually running a campaign to get Terry off air, but they were making it clear they thought the time had come for him to go. All the old affection that had once surrounded him seemed to have disappeared. Terry himself was the first to realise the show should come to an end and actually asked the BBC to release him from his contract, which the BBC refused to do – and then axed the show anyway. It was no way to treat one of its most successful stars.

And when it was announced that the show was to be taken off in 1992 – ironically, to be replaced with the uniquely awful soap opera *El Dorado,* which hardly lasted any time at all – there was almost a feeling of triumph in some quarters that Terry had been forced out. Most celebrities in this country are on the receiving end of a backlash at some point or another: this was Terry's turn.

Even his erstwhile supporters deserted him. '*Wogan* did not quite match up to my expectations of it,' said Michael Grade. 'Though undoubtedly a success, it never achieved importance as one of those rare programmes you must catch or your day will not be complete. It should have been the show everyone rushed home to watch, but it never created that kind of buzz. I knew we were in trouble the first time I called into the production office. On the wall was a huge blackboard with all the shows for the following two months listed, and beneath each date a full complement of guests were set out, each booked in advance. The show was set in concrete.' Of course, it had lasted for seven years, no mean feat in itself, but that cutting-edge feel had undoubtedly been lacking, especially towards the end.

This was almost certainly the beginning of Terry's real disillusionment with the BBC. At its prime, his television show had not only topped the ratings, but also had been receiving 3,000 letters a week, a massive success by any standards. To have treated him with so little dignity did not reflect well on the Corporation and Terry felt it badly at the time. 'Everyone gets axed,' he said many years later.

'Esther Rantzen did *That's Life* for 12 or 15 years and got axed. As far as *Wogan* is concerned, I think the BBC were very ham-fisted about it, but then the BBC were never very good about publicity. It's not a thing they do. They're a corporation and, if you're useful to them, they'll employ you. They're like any other big business – when they've used you up, out you go. It's the same all over.'

True as this is, even in that fevered industry some people deserve to be treated with respect. Terry was one. Even if he never made another programme in his life, that show had made television history and placed Terry in the pantheon of the TV greats. He had become one of the best-known figures in the country, with his interviews sometimes making headline news. He had shown that it was possible to have a chat show that was not hosted by Michael Parkinson, and when his show came to an end he should have been lauded for a great televisual triumph.

The real trouble was that in Britain there is a tendency to cut very successful figures down to size, and that is exactly what happened to Terry. The BBC should have been above it: instead, it all but tossed him to one side.

But, back then, Terry himself was aware that he had outstayed his welcome. That brilliant sense of timing had deserted him: he had been in the right place when the show began, but had failed to realise when it was time to walk away. He had left them wanting less, not more, and he knew it. He brooded about it too.

'*Wogan* was the only thing I didn't time right,' he said. 'And I didn't because I was earning so much money from it. So, instead of following my instinct, which I'd always done before, in *Come Dancing* or *Blankety Blank,* and stopping it when I thought I'd done enough, I let it go on for a year or two years too long.' It was not a lesson he was ever to lose sight of again.

6

MR EUROVISION

'This man is loved in Great Britain and hated in greater continental Europe. When commenting on the Song Contest, Wogan will leave no stone unturned regarding the organising country, the presenters and their outfits, the songs and the final results of the show. He considers it funny and so do the British, who have started to watch the Eurovision more and more every year because of his ironic remarks. Booze has its effect on Wogan, who becomes more and more intolerable as the show develops.'

Press release by the Estonian Eurovision
Song Contest organisers, 2002

The year was 1955. Europe had begun its recovery from the war that had nearly torn it to shreds and which had ended a decade earlier and, as those old wounds began to heal, an audacious plan was hatched. Why not bring the countries of Europe together, in an organisation that would ensure that we never saw Europe-wide hostilities again? It had never been done before, but a new mood of optimism was sweeping the continent, carrying with it goodwill and a desire for change. Heavyweight thinkers gave the plan their support, doubts were raised and silenced, the British were cautious and initially refused to co-operate – and so the Eurovision Song Contest was born.

Its roots actually lay in the San Remo music festival of the 1950s and the competition itself was the brainwave of a Frenchman, Marcel Baison. It was a revolutionary idea at the time. To bring Europe together through a love of music was an ambitious aim indeed, but the world was changing almost overnight, and so why not develop a contest that would be a symbol of these changes? The name 'Eurovision' was actually coined by a journalist whose identity has been lost in the mists of time, but in the beginning, at least, it was taken very seriously by all concerned.

The first contest took place in 1956 at the Teatro Kursaal, in Lugano, Switzerland. It was a far cry from what it is now: seven countries competed, each putting forward two performers. As with that other famous European organisation, the EU, Britain was slow to join in: it was not until 1957 that Patricia Bredin represented the country with 'All', a little number that, at one minute and 50 seconds, remains the shortest Eurovision entry to this day. She performed in Frankfurt and came seventh. There was no British entry in 1958, but since then the UK has been represented every year.

Despite the country's reputation for producing some of the most outstanding musicians of the 1960s, it was a long time before a British Eurovision winner emerged. The first, Sandie Shaw, came a decade after the first UK entry, with 'Puppet on a String', a song that she famously performed barefoot and is said to despise, but which nevertheless has been extremely successful throughout the world and is still regularly played. She was the first of a number of British entrants who were to gain worldwide fame, although perhaps the most successful winners ever were, of course, a Swedish group – Abba. But those joys were yet to come.

The qualification for entry is that the country must be a member of the European Broadcasting Union, which explains the entries put forward by countries whose links with Europe might be spiritual but are certainly not geographical. Lebanon, for example, has been involved in the past, albeit with an unsuccessful entry. And Israel is regularly represented, with some of its entries in recent years attracting global attention.

The Eurovision machinery first cranks into its annual action in Britain each February. This is when *A Song For Europe,* the programme which chooses the British entry, starts to be broadcast, although it has changed its format of late, as we'll see later. A shortlist of songs is chosen by a panel of experts, which is then put to a telephone vote by the audience. The winner becomes the British entry and the contest itself is broadcast in May. It may be a byword for naffness, but it remains hugely popular, generating a sincere feeling that national pride is at stake here: a really good year, or a really dud entry, can provoke either euphoria or soul-searching for the country on whose behalf the entry was made. The worst disgrace is to receive 'nul point' (ever logical, the French is singular: literally, 'not one point') in the course of the evening – a fate that has finally befallen Britain in recent years.

The hosts on the night speak in French and English and the proceedings kick off with a video about the host country, a feature which has itself become something of a talking point for connoisseurs of kitsch. Every country has its own presenters and its own coverage, although it is possible, using satellite and cable, for some viewers to tune in to the show as broadcast by another country. This means that sometimes one country hears what it isn't supposed to and quite a row can ensue – the entire Danish nation has still not forgotten the insults it overheard from Terry's lips. After the songs comes the famous allocation of points, with every country awarding ten other countries points from one to twelve. This is where the dreaded 'nul point' comes in.

Even before Terry's involvement, the contest was associated with a fair amount of nonsense. In 1969, the Norwegian entry was a complete flop, something that country blamed on opposition to its practice of seal culling. More sane voices pointed out that the real problem was that the song, 'Oj, Oj, Oj' (Oi, Oi, Oi), sung by Kirsty Sparboe, was one of the most banal entries in the history of the show. In that same year, an aspiring young singer attempted to represent the UK but failed at the first hurdle. His name? Elton John.

In the event, Lulu, singing 'Boom Bang-A-Bang', was Britain's entry for that year: she was the joint winner with three other countries, the only time this has ever happened, and a severe embarrassment for that year's organisers – European harmony is one thing, but the show is supposed to produce an outright winner. And Elton is not the only singer whose subsequent stature rather belied his performance at the time: a year earlier, Cliff Richard made it into the contest with 'Congratulations', which became a massive hit and is now commonly assumed to have been the winner that year, when in fact it was beaten by a Spanish number which used the word 'la' 138 times. Its title? 'La La La'.

It is a moot point quite which are the worst songs ever performed on Eurovision, but there have certainly been plenty to choose from. Someone once put together a list of the five most awful song titles: they are 'Diggi-Loo Diggi-Ley' by Herreys (Sweden 1984), 'Pump Pump' by Fredi and Friends (Finland 1976), 'Ding Ding Dong' by Teach-in (Holland 1975), 'Bra Vibrationer' by Kikki Danielsson (Sweden 1985) and 'Boum-badaboum' by Minouche Barelli (Monaco 1967). But, in the end, individual taste alone can dictate which song may be deemed the most awful so far performed.

All in all, there could scarcely be a more perfect vehicle for an Irishman with a sardonic wit to host, and it was not long after he started to become well known that Terry became involved with the televised contest. Like so much else he did, it required a quick wit, an ability to think on his feet, a finely honed sense of the ridiculous and a thorough enjoyment of the nonsensical element to the show. He was the perfect choice as presenter and, along with *Children in Need,* the *Eurovision Song Contest* is his longest-running gig on television to date.

Terry's annual outing on the show has now become something of a cult pastime in itself. The audience adore it. Again, a quick wit is required, along with a knack for repartee. Terry is completely irreverent: on one famous occasion, when a woman in an unfeasibly tight outfit appeared on the show, he remarked that he would have liked to make a comment on the song he'd just heard, but he was too distracted. Everyone has their own favourite Terry on *Eurovision* moment: he is now as much of a reason to tune in as any of the songs.

His sardonic commentary has become famous throughout the world, with some countries less enamoured of it than others, but the sarcasm didn't show from the start. Even Terry took the show seriously the first time he was asked to present it: ironically, given that he has become so closely associated with the British entry, his first appearance was actually in Ireland, just a couple of years after he'd emigrated to the UK, in 1971.

Back then, it was very different. The competition was still on a very small scale, for, although the idea had caught on from the start, it was not the big, international event it was later to become. 'When I did my first one at the Gaiety Theatre in Dublin, it was a lovely little place that held about 200 or 300 people,' said Terry in 2002. 'The compere did it from a little box at the side of the tiny stage. Last year, there were 35,000 people in a football ground in Copenhagen. My wife says they were walking up and down the aisles selling vodka shots.'

Naturally, Eurovision has changed just as society has. In the 1950s, the whole world was parochial: now it seems that sophistication is everywhere you look. And in recent years the contest has been given an added energy by the new entrants, the countries that were part of the old Soviet empire and for this reason were not, for many decades, allowed to take part. But it is also much more commercial. Big money is involved these days, whereas 30 years ago it was still a small-scale event. And, as the competition has taken itself ever more seriously, so Terry has done the opposite. He pricks the bubble of pomposity, for British viewers, at least, that threatens to pervade the show.

Terry was not to take over as the annual compere until 1980, but from 1971 onwards he began hosting the show on an ad hoc basis, being there for some of the most memorable moments of them all. In 1974, Abba won with 'Waterloo', which not only became an international hit but also launched the singing career of one of the most famous pop groups of all time. (It is widely forgotten that they had tried to enter the previous year with 'Ring Ring' but failed at Sweden's selection stage.)

All in all, 1974 was quite a year. The Italian entry, 'Si', was deemed highly controversial in its home country: it was banned from Italian television screens for several days after the contest because broadcasters were worried that it might influence the outcome of a referendum to be held on whether to legalise divorce. Meanwhile, the Portuguese offering, sung by Paulo de Cavalho, achieved a greater distinction still: it became the only Eurovision entry ever to trigger a revolution, when the troops' sign to start overthrowing the government came with the opening bars of 'E Depois Do Adeus' (And After Goodbye). There was drama up there on the stage as well: another presenter that year was Katie Boyle. Panic ensued when the producers realised her underwear would be visible on stage to the audience: she was forced to remove it and protect her modesty with the strategic use of prompt cards.

It was a mixture of the sublime and the ridiculous, of revolution and not quite the right underwear. It's amazing that so many countries do still take it seriously: every year there is some preventable crisis, some ludicrous entry, some unfortunate who scores '*nul point*'. But the opportunity for comedy is enormous. It would be tempting to suspect that sometimes an attempt is made to sabotage the show, but, if truth be told, the possibility for chaos is always present, with no necessity for an outside agent to get involved.

It was a natural environment for Terry to become involved with, and he took to it like the proverbial duck to water. The two could have been made for each other, and thanks once again to that early training on RTE he found himself well able to cope. The show does not have a script and it is Terry's opinion that it would not work as well if it did. 'I ad lib it all,' he said. 'That's the way I work all the time, on radio and television. We go to rehearsals, of course, because you have to see what's going to happen and we have to find out what the timings are. You don't want to be speaking when the song is starting. You need to be able to synchronise what you're saying to what the public is seeing and hearing. At the first rehearsal I think, This sounds like utter rubbish, when I hear the songs, but by the third hearing I think, I like that, it's quite good! Music is all about repetition, though.'

It didn't take long for the irreverence to creep in, though, much to the delight of the viewers and the disgust of the other countries taking part. But even in the UK there were a few people who didn't get the joke: in 1989, the United Kingdom Eurovision Song Contest fan club expressed upset that Terry constantly took the mick. 'His jibes are not wanted,' they said. 'He should take the show more seriously.'

Terry himself was unperturbed. 'Listen, anybody who takes this show seriously in the United Kingdom should be banjaxed,' he said. It is a view the vast majority of the viewers share: most people do not turn on the television on the night of the *Eurovision Song Contest* hoping to hear some radical new music announced with gravitas. They tune in to hear Terry becoming ruder and ruder about the caterwauling taking place on stage, and he never fails to please.

And he is certainly given plenty of material to work with. The lyrics of the average Eurovision song are dire. The costumes, on the whole, should be made illegal. Some entered the public consciousness: Bucks Fizz, in particular, once created a move that is still remembered by millions of a certain age: the two men whipped off the skirts of the two women, to reveal a shorter garment underneath. It was incredibly innocent by today's standards, but caused a sensation – and pages of press coverage – at the time.

Indeed, it was difficult to watch the proceedings without reflecting on the unintentional humour. In 1990, the contest took place in the newly liberated Yugoslavia, the first erstwhile communist country to host the show. Chaos promptly ensued. The total cost of staging the event was £5 million, which seems a piffling sum now for an international television extravaganza, but it was almost beyond the purse strings of the host nation.

This in turn led to more embarrassment, when it emerged that tickets were being sold on the black market to help fund the show. The organisers in Zagreb belatedly realised they needed sponsorship to help with the costs: some of the sponsors, however, decided to regain their own contribution by selling on the tickets. And then it transpired that there weren't enough tickets for the concert hall to go round in the first place because of a massive miscalculation about the amount of space involved.

'The original estimate of seats meant nothing, because they hadn't realised that the stage set, the cameras and the commentary booths meant removing a huge chunk of seats,' said a member of the Irish contingent, somehow managing to keep a straight face. But then chaos is what helps drive the show forward: half the fun every year is waiting to see what will go wrong next.

That was also the year that Eurovision got a facelift. It had, after all, been going for 35 years by that stage and so some much-needed improvements were brought in: inane dance routines were out and solo contestants were in. 'We are trying to make the contest more fashionable,' said a deeply optimistic spokesman. 'We have encouraged established songwriters to take us more seriously, and there definitely seems to be a move away from the "Boom Bang-A-Bang" style of Eurovision songs.'

Terry himself remained completely unmoved by all the upheaval around him. Long ago he had decided where his main concerns lay when presenting the show. 'Our priorities are essentially the restaurants,' he once said. 'The producer sends me the menus in advance. As far as we're concerned, that's it. We go on Thursday, there's the commentators' briefing, which we never attend. We go out to dinner. It's wonderful. After the contest, there's always a party and it's usually terrible. They never spend enough money and there's far too many people. We never go to that, either.'

In many ways, it was just as well he kept a distance between himself and the main organisers of the show, for his very presence seemed to mock the proceedings, before he had even said a word. The British sense of humour is well known to delight in the ridiculous, and there was little more ridiculous than a group of flamboyantly dressed, often second-(or third-)rate singers taking themselves very seriously – something that deeply amused both Terry and the audience. Nor did he confine himself to barbed wit when the show was actually on: he provided a commentary on the proceedings right from the moment the choice of British entry had begun, both on *A Song For Europe* and via his various other media outlets.

And, as the years passed, his propensity for upsetting people only deepened. He was unafraid not only to criticise the host countries and the proceedings, but also the British element. In 1993, he voiced concerns in public about that year's entry, saying that the pop star Sonia had been saddled with the wrong song in 'Better the Devil You Know'. 'Sonia is a fabulous woman and a great performer, but I don't think our song is up to it,' he said. 'With the right song, I think Sonia would stroll it. But I simply don't think this one is good enough to win.' But who better to comment on the British entries than Terry? After all, he has been associated with the show for over 30 years.

And the Eurovision Song Contest, for all its naffness, has been the launching pad for some serious talent. The most famous example is Abba, but other people have founded highly successful careers on the back of it, and one of these is the dancer Michael Flatley. Originally from Chicago, Flatley appeared in the 1994 contest in a five-minute slot featuring a modern rock interpretation of Irish dance: the performance was so successful that it was extended to a full-length piece: *Riverdance.*

By 1995, Terry was coming clean about his real feelings towards the show itself, rather than simply those taking part. It had been pretty clear to everyone for some time now that he didn't think it was the most earth-shattering event of the year, but now all the cards were on the table. It was to be held in Dublin that year – the very place where Terry had first presented the show, although the proceedings had changed somewhat in the intervening years – and finally he could hold his tongue no longer.

'This whole thing was set up to bring the nations of Europe together and it has failed miserably,' he said. 'It needs a good kick into touch. Every other country takes it very seriously but I think the British are mature enough to realise it's only a song contest rather than an extension of national pride. If truth be known, it's a major blow to unity. Even the Irish take it seriously – Lord knows why – it's just music, not brain surgery.'

This remark prompted a bit of a sense of humour failure among the Irish. There has been some resentment from his fellow countrymen over the years as he has seemed to ally himself more closely with the British than the people from whom he came, and this was one occasion on which they felt compelled to answer back. Larry Gogan, RTE's top disc jockey, was not amused.

'I'm afraid the British pop scene is out of tune with everyone else,' he said. 'It's plainly obvious the BBC want to win it again. Terry has become famous for his annual slagging off of the Eurovision Song Contest, but he enjoys it every year. Anyway, for the past few years it has given him a free trip home to Ireland to see the family. Sorry, Terry, I couldn't resist my national pride showing.'

Pat Kenney, a former Irish host of the contest, agreed. 'I'm afraid Terry and his BBC colleagues already know once again that their song hasn't a chance of winning,' he said. 'I feel that Britain is at odds with Europe over most things so why should their entries for Eurovision be any different? Terry is already admitting Britain hasn't a hope in hell of winning the contest.' Terry, needless to say, was unmoved.

But he did admit that there was the odd tension with his fellow countrymen, due not so much to Eurovision itself as to the fact that he had lived in the UK so long now that he identified with it. 'Oh, I am Irish,' he said, when asked why he referred to the British as 'we' during *Eurovision.* 'Sometimes the Irish get very annoyed when I say, "we", referring to the UK, but I have lived here for over 30 years.

'Two of my children were born here. They all have Irish passports and see themselves as Irish. They love the Irish but they wouldn't live in Ireland any more than I would. It drives me mad, second-and third-generation Irish saying, "I'm away home for the holidays." I think, Home? What are you talking about? Home is where your family are.'

Terry certainly regarded Britain as home by this stage, and the compliment was repaid in full. It was, after all, Britain that had made him who he was today. Had he stayed in Ireland, he would almost certainly have become as famous there as he is in Britain, but it is very unlikely his fame would have extended to other shores. As it is, Terry has had a platform in Britain for decades from which to make his views known. And one of the reasons why that state of affairs has come about is because he has become so well known for presenting *Eurovision.* It is hardly surprising he identified with the country that had been his home for so long.

There were, however, moments of glory. In 1997, the British entry, 'Love Shine a Light', by Katrina and the Waves, took the prize. At 227 points, it set a record for the UK entry and, despite all the carping, the country is the joint-second highest overall winner, having by 2005 won five times, to equal France and Luxembourg. Only Ireland has done better, with seven wins. The UK has also finished second a record 17 times, with Terry gloating over the proceedings all the way.

As the years have passed, Terry has become increasingly sardonic, which for some viewers continues to be a reason to tune into the show. One memorable quip came in 1998: 'Twelve points from Slovakia to Malta really restores your faith in the chaos theory, doesn't it?' And his comments became ever more biting as the evening wore on, helped by the consumption of something with a nip to it. Connoisseurs of the programme even enjoyed comparing Terry's commentary in the early and the later parts of the evening. It all added to the fun.

Terry himself has become increasingly open about his propensity for taking refreshment while the show is going on: 'Bailey's Irish Cream, with ice, in my commentary box,' he admits. 'It's a dairy product, very good for you, you can't do without it. I get halfway through every year and I think, Are we ever going to make it to the end? This is awful. But then I'm usually half-drunk. Everybody watching is too.

'All those enormous Eurovision parties, enormously camp. Richard Curtis has one. And Lenny Henry too.'

And it is not only the rich and famous who have Eurovision parties: they have become something of a nationwide phenomenon – much as *Dallas* parties once were, when viewers would match the Ewing family, especially JR, with a drink taken at home for every one imbibed on the screen.

There was also great excitement in 1998, with the first-ever transsexual contestant, Dana International, who went on to win the contest. Named in honour of the Irish winner Dana, who had appeared in the 1970 contest, Dana International, who was from Israel, caused an absolute sensation. She was not universally admired, and perhaps least of all by some of her compatriots, who protested against her participation on religious grounds. Eventually, she had to be given a dressing room with bulletproof windows and an armed guard. But, again, it is of these moments, incomparable in their naffness, that the show is made.

And for all the nonsense, this episode did illustrate that Eurovision has a wider impact than would at first seem to be the case. The fuss about Dana International actually overshadowed the competition itself, given how much attention was paid to her gender. Nonetheless, the show is capable of sparking national debate and soul-searching, especially when a 'nul point' moment comes along. It is watched with an eagle eye by the record industry and attracts millions of viewers every year. It is a serious event, for all that is ridiculous about the proceedings on the night.

Terry remembers with a certain amount of glee the highlights of the vast number of competitions he's been party to. Asked if there would ever be a better entry than 'My Lovely Horse', he replied, 'No. "My Lovely Horse" should be an entry every year. And if we could possibly have some striptease going on, and some people playing Xena the Warrior Princess, that would probably be a winner. And if it came to the Balkans...'

By the start of the 21st century, Terry had become a national icon as far as presenting *Eurovision* is concerned. And one of the reasons that he has been so enduring as a host is that he has never taken the programme seriously. Several decades after he started presenting it, neither, finally, according to him, do we. 'At last the British public have got the joke,' said Terry on the eve of the contest in May 2001. 'They're the only ones in Europe who have. Everybody else takes it terribly seriously. Even in Ireland, where there is wonderful cynicism, they think it's a song contest rather than an exercise in foolishness.'

In Terry's opinion, the whole event has become an exercise in European *realpolitik,* especially now that so many smaller European countries have been allowed to join in. Europe might want to pretend it's a homogeneous mass, but in reality the old divisions are as strong as ever. 'The idea is a wonderful one,' he said. 'Bringing everybody in Europe together. But all it makes manifestly clear is how far apart we are. Prejudice, bias, chauvinism.

'Denmark will always vote for Iceland. Iceland will always vote for Denmark. Greece will always vote for Cyprus. Cyprus will always give 12 marks to Greece. And none to Turkey. And nobody gives the UK anything, because they don't like us. The reason Ireland wins so often is that it's little Ireland. Never invaded anybody. The French? How many votes do you think we're going to get from France this year? I tell you now. None. And we won't get any from Ireland, either.' (Note that Terry was again identifying himself here with England, not Ireland.)

He's probably right. Some unspeakably awful songs have been known to do quite well; other quite good numbers have sunk without a trace. The smaller countries do sometimes appear to be sucking up to the larger ones, and it's certainly true that Ireland tends to do very well. But then again, so does Britain. For all that we might have upset our European partners from time to time, Britain hasn't done badly out of the competition at all – another triumph for Britain and its role in Europe, perhaps.

Terry doesn't see it that way. His point-blank refusal ever to take it seriously knows no bounds. Asked what the cultural value of Eurovision is, and what his favourite entry is, he replied, 'All I've gained by watching the Eurovision Song Contest over the years is a numbing of the prefrontal lobes. Traditionally, about ten seconds after the contest has finished every year, I've forgotten every song in it, so I'll have to say that my favourite has been Abba's "Waterloo", as that is the only one I can remember. It used to be that whatever won the Eurovision went on to become an international hit, but not any more. People have more sense than that now. The whole thing has become an astounding, huge, grandiose load of rubbish.'

He could be pretty scathing about the way in which the British entry is picked too. 'Even a *nul point* situation? It could be this year,' he said in 2001. 'No, we do continue to pick the wrong song. Last year, two old geezers, who were too old for Radio 2, won the thing with some kind of dingy old ballad. And what did we pick this year? This 16-year-old disco queen, a fella doing scratch records in the background. What is this going to mean in Estonia? Nothing. For goodness sake!'

That was also the year when he managed to cause real offence – to the entire citizenry of Denmark, who found his commentary on the night just too over the top. 'It's a tribute to how good Danish television is that a lot of the Danish public were watching on BBC satellite and listening to me,' Terry said smoothly afterwards. 'I was sending it up in the same way I always do, but the Danes are sensitive. So they take any criticism as criticism of Denmark, which is undoubtedly the finest country in the world. The result was I got inundated with emails from Denmark saying, "So, you cocksucker, you think..." I was getting fantastic abuse, dog's abuse.'

He had, though, very nearly gone too far, for the first time ever. 'There are people who obviously think that I don't take it seriously enough – certainly, the Danes took exception to me last year,' he said one year on. 'They'd been listening to my commentary on BBC Prime and there I was, on the front pages of the Danish newspapers, because of what they took to be my offensive comments about their presenters. These two comperes came out and did the whole contest in English, in rhyming couplets. I called them Dr Death and the Tooth Fairy and, for some reason, they took great exception.' The British viewers had, in fact, been tremendously amused throughout, but so annoyed was Denmark that the BBC even considered issuing an apology.

In the end, common sense prevailed. Part of the point of Eurovision these days is Terry's sarcasm, and if other countries fail to get the joke – well, then, the joke's on them. The people of Denmark made themselves look a little bit oversensitive with their angst, just as other countries have done in the past. In fact, it could be taken as a badge of honour to be insulted by Terry. It takes imagination and energy to think up these putdowns and they tend to be remembered long after the actual contest has been consigned to the more obscure vaults of memory.

In 2003, there was a huge upset in Britain, when the contest was held in Latvia, although its location was not the problem. Terry's version of *realpolitik* again came into play. 'The Baltic states have taken over,' he said. 'They vote for their next-door neighbours because that's what they had to do when they were under the paw of the Russian bear. I wouldn't be surprised if Russia or Lithuania wins this year. It's in the nature of people to vote for people they like, which is why the UK gets no votes.' He spoke more truly than he realised.

For the first time in Eurovision history, Britain scored '*nul point*' for Jemini singing a song penned by Martin Isherwood, the head of music at Sir Paul McCartney's Liverpool Academy, provoking widespread changes in the way the programme was to be presented. Until now, *A Song for Europe* had been stashed away on Sunday afternoons when no one watched it: the BBC, looking and learning from the success of programmes like *Pop Idol*, decided to revamp it under the title *Eurovision: Making Your Mind Up,* echoing Bucks Fizz's success in 1981, which was to go out on prime time on Saturday nights. Apart from anything else, this would ensure a different (and younger) viewing audience, which would in turn result in the choice of a different kind of song.

Jemini themselves – Chris Cromby and Gemma Abbey – behaved with good grace after the event. 'We tried our hardest,' said Chris. 'We had a great time and, as far as we are concerned, we gave one of the best performances ever, but I guess it was just one of those things. We had a few technical problems. One of the monitors went, which meant that Gemma could not hear herself; it just wasn't our night.' Terry himself blamed the result on a post-Iraq backlash whereby the other countries competing didn't want to vote for the UK.

And, again, it was a mark of the fact that Eurovision is held in sneaking regard in this country that the whole episode was seen as a blow to national pride. Britain may feel it is above the proceedings – but it still wants to win. Equally, when Britain does well, there tends to be national celebration afterwards. We are not quite as blasé a nation as we like to think.

And, while Terry might not be universally popular throughout Europe, that year's contest proved that it was not only Britain that appreciated his talents. Australia did too, and there was an outcry when the show went out in Oz with an Australian presenter, Des Mangan, rather than Terry. Viewers were so irate that they jammed the Australian channel SBS's switchboard with complaints, forcing it to run the show again, but this time with Terry fronting it. 'His cynical comments are the reason many Australians watch it,' said one insider, another adding, 'The *Eurovision* without Wogan is like a barbie without cold beer. It was a complete flop.'

And Terry continues to go from strength to strength. But the show has tossed up some odd anomalies: although it is not going too far to call him the face of *Eurovision,* in Britain, at least, it is the only television he's done in which he's never actually appeared on screen. But that is almost irrelevant: Terry is now so well known that viewers can imagine him talking directly to them, even if they can only hear his voice.

'All I'm really doing is anticipating the viewers' comments,' he avers. 'If I say, "Those are serious teeth," then that is what's going through the public's minds at the very same time. The majority of people – not everybody – tend to identify with me and my view of Eurovision.' That is true, and the public enjoy the fact that whatever they are thinking at home tends to be expressed, via Terry, on national TV. It makes them feel part of the contest on an individual level. It makes them feel almost as if they are there.

It is exactly the same talent that made his talk show work so well. As has been stated before, Terry is the bridge between the celebrity and the man in the street, the event and the viewer, the incident and the comment it gives rise to in millions of homes. Who has not shouted a comment at the screen and then heard Terry say much the same directly afterwards? It reflects how closely he relates to the views of the viewers, just as he does to listeners to his radio show, that he says almost exactly what they think.

Despite the length of time that he's been presenting the contest, though, Terry maintains that he has never been able to pick the winner in advance. 'I'm always sent a tape beforehand and I'll make up my mind who's going to win and go round to the bookies and put a couple of quid on – I always lose though,' he said in 2002. 'You just can't second-guess it, but that's part of the fun and the outrage and the madness. Last year, one of the jurors said, "And so we give the 12 points to our neighbours, Slovenia." You just think, That's not what it's about. It's a song contest. It's not about showing what good neighbours you are.'

And Terry continued to waver between patriotic fervour for the old country and a pragmatic support for the new one. In 2002, Ireland was not in the contest, which saddened him – indeed, for once he spoke out on behalf of his compatriots, rather than the British. To begin with, that is. 'The sadness, this year, for me, is that Ireland has been relegated,' he said. 'How would you feel if you'd won about five times in succession, more than anybody else, and you were relegated? That's a strange rule. You can get relegated unless you're the UK, Germany or Spain. They made the mistake of relegating Germany a couple of years ago and then found their funds considerably depleted.'

But, when push came to shove, Terry was back with the British. Terry can be extremely pragmatic when it comes down to it: emotion plays a secondary role. He was aware where his interests lay. 'Who's paying my fee?' he asked. 'I'm the representative of the BBC; I'm the representative of the UK entry. I don't cheer for Ireland, although I may be delighted if they win. It's like Peter O'Sullevan, the racing commentator. When he commentated on the Grand National or the Derby and he had a horse running in it, he didn't start cheering for his own horse!' It was a telling comment. Terry was very well aware how much he owed to being the British face of *Eurovision:* he wasn't about to let the side down.

In 2004, the year after the '*nul point*' debacle, Terry rose to the challenge of expressing Britain's hopes for the future and managed to say how concerned he was about how it would all go now. 'I am sick with worry for our chances,' he confessed. 'We're still the victim of prejudicial voting because of Tony Blair and the war. Everybody hates Britain at the moment.' He was also diplomatic about James Fox, who had already appeared in *Fame Academy* and was now the UK's entrant.

'A lot of people are championing James as a modern-day Cliff Richard, which might sound like a vicious insult, but in Eurovision terms it's one of the highest compliments you can be paid,' he said. 'The highest, of course, is being compared to Abba. If it wasn't for the politics, he'd walk it because pop music is naturally anglicised. I mean, have you ever heard French domestic pop music? It's hideous.'

In the event, James came 16th, while the voting became even more blatant than ever. 'You could write all these votes down in advance,' he said, as one neighbouring country after another awarded points to their allies. 'It was beyond a joke. Insane! Farcical!'

The following year, 2005, the British entry was Javine, singing 'Touch My Fire'. Some Eurovision experts gloomily pointed out that the second entrant of the evening had never yet been a winner and Javine, of course, came on stage second. She ended up finishing third from the bottom, while Greece won, helped by a 12-point award from Cyprus. This time round, Terry couldn't even be bothered to feign outrage: he contented himself by pointing out that the countries that came bottom – the UK, France, Germany and Spain – were also the major financial contributors to the event. Perhaps, too, we were victims of the jealousy of other countries that night.

If we were, Terry would have delighted in it. Other television shows come and go, but he says he is determined to stick with this one. '*Eurovision* or *Children in Need* – that's different,' he says. 'They'll have to drag me away screaming. I will not relinquish those easily. They'll have to shoot me. *Eurovision* is without flaw. It is magnificent in its stupidity. Grandiose rubbish.'

And certainly it looks as if he will be presenting the show for the foreseeable future. When the BBC thinks it needs to up the glamour content, it does so by way of his sidekick – in 2005, *Eurovision: Making Your Mind Up* was co-hosted by Natasha Kaplinsky – but it knows it has in Terry not only a gem but also someone who is so closely associated with *Eurovision* in the public mind that it would be madness to let him go. He clearly has no desire to, either. It is to be hoped there will be very many Terry-presented *Eurovision* years ahead.

7

TERRYVISION

As time moved on and Terry seemed to appear just about everywhere, inevitably his success translated into material wealth. The Wogans have for a long time lived in a very comfortable house in Berkshire, with its own grounds and swimming pool, and have added a few more properties to their portfolio, including a holiday home in Gascony, in the south of France. In earlier times, they had a place in Spain. They do not, however, own a property in Ireland. But Terry, while enjoying his now considerable wealth, has always been adamant that money alone is not the reason that he does what he does. But he does like what it brings him.

Back in 1990, when he was still presenting *Wogan* three times a week, Terry came under some scrutiny when he signed a new two-year deal with the BBC said to be worth £1 million. He was coy about it all. 'I don't like to discuss money,' he said. 'But you should never go into anything thinking about the money you're going to make out of it. I don't mind admitting that, as soon as I could afford to pay someone to mow the lawn, I paid them. That's what money is for, to provide you with the comforts of life if you're lucky enough. What you should be doing is looking for something that you love to do. That's what makes you successful.'

Those were wise words. Terry has been very well rewarded over the course of the years, something he himself is happy to admit, but he did not pick his career for the money he would earn. Radio and television performers do tend to be very well paid when they are working, but the big risk is that there can be extended periods when there is no gainful employment to be had. Terry has been exceedingly lucky in this respect: he has never been out of work. Most people in his profession cannot say the same, and that includes some of the biggest stars in the land.

Nor did he go into it with the express intention of being famous. In these days of reality television, when people appear on the box purely to become well known, and no matter that they have no perceptible talent to get them there, it is easy to forget that some of the most famous people in the country became famous because they were so good at what they did. For Terry has risen massively above the ranks of even his fellow DJs and television presenters. His is now the kind of fame that almost makes him seem part of the family: for many people, it is impossible to remember a time when he hasn't been around.

Of course, this will not continue forever, but it is now up to Terry to decide when he wants to go. He is in the extremely rare position of being able to time his own exit – inasmuch as anyone ever is – for the simple reason that the BBC is desperate to hang on to him. Terry is no longer a full-time BBC employee – he is a freelancer – but he is far and away the most successful DJ in the country and his departure will cause a major headache for the heads of the BBC.

Unlike so many others in the world of celebrity, Terry has never made the mistake of believing his own publicity. But he has been canny enough to understand what lies behind his success. 'What I've been good at, so far, is anticipating trends,' he said in the early 1990s. 'When I left Ireland to come and work here, I just thought the time was right. The same thing happened when I took over the Radio 2 morning show. That could have been a failure for me, but it wasn't. Then I took over *Blankety Blank* on TV – that could have been a disaster. I decided to give up *Blankety Blank* when I felt it had run its course, and started doing the talk show.'

This was when *Wogan* was at its height, of course: there were as yet no plans to axe it and Terry remained the undisputed gem in the BBC's crown. There was even talk of extending the show further. 'It doesn't matter who does it, five nights a week is going to be done one day,' said Terry. 'Without false modesty, it's a tough brief doing a talk show at 7pm. Most talk shows go out at about 11pm, but I've never wanted to broadcast in a vacuum. This is why I was glad when people like Ben Elton took over my show.

And Jonathan Ross will be doing it when I'm on holiday this summer.'

That has been another good Terry trick: never appear desperate to hang on to your show. Some presenters can be extremely prickly about handing over the reins, even for a short time, to someone else: the ever-present fear is that they will do the job better and the initial presenter's career will be a thing of the past. All this does in the longer term is to show their insecurity, which is, in the words of a showbiz insider, 'never a good look'. Far better to appear so utterly unconcerned about the competition that you scarcely notice it is there: in show business, as in dating, it simply makes you more attractive to those all around.

It is a trait to be seen to this day: Terry is well known for the amount of holiday he takes, and he appears supremely unconcerned about how the show will fare when he is away. He comes across as vaguely hoping that the listeners will miss him, but at the same time fully aware that there are more important things in life. He has never been shy about estimating his own worth, however, and for very many years now has insisted on being paid well for his work. That, combined with careful saving and investing, means that he doesn't actually need to work now, and hasn't needed to for years. It has put him in the enviable position of being able to pick and choose his projects. He is not in a position where he has to hang on.

And, for many years, he has had absolutely nothing to prove. He has won every award worth winning, trumped the opposition and now, as the final accolade, ended up as a knight of the realm. Indeed, Terry professed supreme contentment when it came to looking towards the future. 'I don't worry at all,' he said. 'I've never been out of work. I'm not insecure. I don't have a game plan. There's very little left for me to do, though, in a sense.'

That was not, however, what everyone thought. Apart from *Wogan* and *Eurovision,* Terry appeared to be on the screen almost non-stop, and another undertaking that he has been involved with for more than two decades is the other show he has always said he will refuse to give up: *Children in Need.*

This event, the BBC's annual appeal for its own charity for children, first came to our screens in 1979 and the following year was broadcast for the first time as a telethon. The presenters of *Children in Need* were Terry, Esther Rantzen and Sue Lawley, and it caught the attention of the public immediately: £1 million was raised, which, back then, was an awful lot of money. The BBC now sets aside an entire evening to broadcast the appeal, which also incorporates events designed to raise money, and the whole lot goes out on BBC1, but for the first few years it was dotted in between other programmes. In 1983, for example, it shared star billing with *The Five Doctors,* a 90-minute *Dr Who* anniversary special.

In fact, the BBC had had a long and honourable history when it came to raising money for disadvantaged children. The very first BBC broadcast to that end went out on the radio on Christmas Day 1927, raising over £1,000, and the programme continued until 1955, when it transferred to BBC TV. And there it stayed until 1979, when it turned into the appeal as we know it today. Almost, that is. These days it is a star-studded event: when it began, as someone once put it, it had a roll call that would have seemed more suited to *Nationwide,* including Henry Cooper, Willy Rushton and Chas and Dave.

The appeal is designed to improve the lives and prospects of children living in the UK who have experienced some kind of hardship. In 1985, another Children in Need regular appeared: Pudsey Bear, a teddy bear with a bandage over one eye. Pudsey's popularity rivalled Terry's and he was soon adopted as a mascot for the show, as well as its official logo. He also appears on Children in Need merchandise, sold to make money for the charity. Events – sponsored sitting in a bath of baked beans is one that comes to mind – raise money for the show and it has become increasingly successful: by its 25th anniversary, held on 19 November 2004, £17 million was raised on the night alone.

In total, Children in Need has now raised over £400 million, and in doing so has thrown up some bizarre moments in its wake. One of these centred on its 25th anniversary: the star prize was a Honda FR-V.

It was, however, rather an unusual car, in that it was covered with signatures of dozens of celebrities: Elton John, Kylie Minogue, Donny Osmond, David Coulthard, Ozzy and Sharon Osbourne, Andrew Marr and Terry himself had all put their mark on the car. It was won by a person who didn't drive – and who three months later put it up for auction.

As ever, Terry turned out to be just the right man for the job. It required an avuncular figure, who could appeal for donations and talk about the children for which the money was needed without being mawkish. It needed someone who could rise to the seriousness of the event but still maintain a sense of fun. Above all, it needed someone who could carry hours and hours of live broadcasting, without tripping up, either literally or metaphorically, who could cope with unexpected crises in the studio and who could still appear fresh at the end of a long evening. Terry was all of those things.

Children in Need has actually been a very influential programme. It was the UK's first-ever telethon, and as such led the way for others: *Comic Relief* first appeared on our screens in 1988, the same year that ITV ran its first telethon. It has also been extremely innovative: one feature was an auction called 'Things That Money Can't Buy'. In 2004, the 25th-anniversary season, these included a private skating party in Hampton Court, a cocktail party with cocktails mixed by Alex Kammerling, the author of *Blend Me, Shake Me,* and the chance to act in a scene from *EastEnders.*

And, like Eurovision, the annual appeal looks set to continue way into the future. It has become an annual event that is looked forward to, combining as it does celebrity, entertainment and the chance to do good. In some senses, it is Terry's baby, in that he was one of the founders of the modern-day version of the appeal, and his opportunity to give something back to a world that has given him so much. He is clearly utterly concerned about the people the charity benefits, and yet he manages to get the message across without the haranguing methods that other stars adopt.

Terry began to take on a whole series of projects that were neither one-offs nor entirely regular. Another hugely popular show that he has been long associated with is *Auntie's Bloomers,* which began back in 1990. It was a direct riposte to ITV: for some years, Denis Norden had been hosting *It'll Be Alright on the Night,* a series of outtakes featuring famous television and film stars fluffing their lines, tripping over the scenery and generally making themselves look idiotic.

With the BBC's huge library of source material stretching back decades, a show along similar lines was a logical undertaking, and who better to front it than Terry? Again, it was an association that was to span more than a decade, turning out to be hugely successful and spawning any number of related shows – *Auntie's Sporting Bloomers, Auntie's Big Bloomers, Auntie's Golden Bloomers, Auntie's Shocking Soccer Bloomers* and others too numerous to mention.

These programmes, while looked down on in some quarters, are actually massively popular television. And, yet again, Terry appears as the person who manages to introduce celebrity to real life. Another funny aspect of his fame is that in some ways he seems to be the supremely normal person: the man next door who by some strange twist of fate has become enormously famous. In presenting the *Bloomers* programmes, he appears to derive just as much enjoyment from the frolics on the screen as the rest of the audience. It never seems to occur to anyone, least of all Terry himself, that he is quite as famous as the people on the screen he is presenting to the rest of us.

And, as with so many of his shows, it is impossible not to wonder, is it suited to Terry or is Terry suited to it? Something else that has aided him in his long career is the ability to make a television show entirely his own. For example, many people tend to think that *Blankety Blank* was specifically developed to showcase Terry's talents; it wasn't. It was based on a US show put together years before. Similarly, *Wogan* was the first show of its kind in the UK, but the concept of a chat-show host appearing several times a week was already long established in the United States. And as for Eurovision – it would have existed whether or not Terry had anything to do with it. But it was an opportunity to put his own thumbprint on it and it became entirely his.

By the mid-1990s, though, it briefly seemed as if *Eurovision* and *Children in Need,* along with series like *Auntie's Bloomers,* were going to be Terry's main reason for appearing on the screen. In the wake of the demise of *Wogan,* he was given an extremely short-lived chat show on Friday nights and, worse still, a planned high-profile interview show called *Wogan Meets* ... was cancelled after just one outing. It was not a happy time – on television, at least.

His disillusionment was beginning to show through. In recent years, Terry has ruffled more than a few feathers at the BBC because of his outspoken criticism of the Corporation, but, in fact, he started sniping at least a decade ago. And who could blame him? Despite the fact that he was still doing a fair bit of television work for the Beeb, it had treated him badly at the end of *Wogan.* At the very least, a dignified exit should have been organised for a performer of his stature; instead, it had come to a nasty and sticky end.

And so with this in the background and a television career that was going through a rough patch, he was not quite the easy-going old Terry the nation had grown to love. To put it bluntly: he was fed up. Talking about his deal with the BBC, which he has never revealed, which bound him exclusively to the Corporation at that time and which has made him a rich man, he said, 'Thank God no one's ever found out exactly what I get. But I think there has got to be a change in paying stars enormous amounts to be under contract. Television is making a mistake of thinking it's them the viewers are watching. It's not, it's the programmes.

'Buying stars and putting them under contract without a show for them is just foolish. That's because people on TV have no real idea what's popular until it's too late. What is discussed and approved over the pine tables of west London is not necessarily what they are talking about up in Heckmondwike. The idea was that the BBC would develop a new string for my bow but, so far, nothing has happened.

'They've offered me a couple of game shows, but I am not interested in those. The odd new challenge would be welcome. They obviously think highly enough of me to pay me an awful lot of money to be exclusive to them, so I hope something will happen soon. Otherwise, I may think about going somewhere else with some new ideas. But that's in the future.'

This was also a time in which there were some problems with his family, which we'll come to later, which added to his disgruntlement – at one point, he even declared that, if this was the price of fame, he would never have left Ireland. But everyone, no matter what their career, has to go through a bad stage, and this was one of his. Terry has also observed in recent years that, since he wasn't interested in cookery or gardening, there was clearly nothing more for him to do on television – although this was to prove to be not quite the case.

He was sounding downright disaffected – although that was not, if truth be told, the whole story. In 1996, when the BBC's Chairman, Marmaduke Hussey, retired, a small and exclusive dinner was held to mark his departure, and Terry, as one of the biggest names at the BBC, was one of the guests. He was indisputably a member of the charmed elite, of that handful of performers who are valued so highly that they have become personal friends with the powers that be. Terry was and is a member of the great and the good and no short-term irritation at the state of television on his part was going to change that.

On his new radio show, of which more later, Terry was already taking the mickey out of the new Chairman, Sir Christopher Bland. 'Actually, he heard me taking the piss on his first day and popped into the studio to see what was going on,' Terry revealed. 'He seemed to think it was funny. Too bad if he didn't.' Terry was clearly not a man who either had been banished from the magical inner circle or was sitting in dread of the people in power now.

Nor was any limitation ever put on the subjects he was allowed to address – hence the constant baiting of whoever happened to be DG. For all his complaints when he was feeling bad-tempered, Terry was accorded complete licence to talk pretty much about whatever he liked. It was a canny move on the part of Radio 2, for not only did Terry appear at his best when he was allowed free reign, but also the BBC's bosses also freed themselves from any charge of pomposity.

And there was no one Terry was worried about upsetting. The Wogan persona meant he was highly unlikely to use bad language on air or choose subject matter that was not to everyone's liking, but Terry's greatest and most effective weapon was to tease. He teased everyone: the great and the good, the silly and the affected, the celebrity of the day, himself, his listeners – everyone. And he did so in such a good-natured way that no one could really take umbrage. It is a talent he has long used to enormous effect.

And he had other considerations to preoccupy him. His children were growing up: Alan and Mark had both been working on television and radio, while Katherine was considering an acting career after she finished university. Terry addressed the issue in his own inimitable fashion. 'I'd be quite nervous of becoming famous these days,' he confessed in 1996. 'The spotlight has become very savage and very unforgiving. Look at poor Michael Barrymore. My example hasn't put my children off. They see me, a more or less untalented oaf, being paid for old rope and how can you blame them?

'But there's no other job that I'd have liked to have had. I have had a terrific career and I'm not finished yet. In about 15 years' time, I'll probably be doing the epilogue on Thames Valley Radio. I'll be known as the Grand Old Man of Broadcasting. You see, the British public have always confused longevity with merit. In the end, they'll think I'm quite good. I expect eventually to be elevated to a kind of legendary status.' Ironic words, but they would seem to have come true by now.

There were plenty of one-off television appearances, sometimes as a presenter and sometimes playing himself in a drama. In 1992, he did the latter in a long-forgotten film called *Born Kicking* and the following year he appeared in *Comic Relief: The Invasion of the Comic Tomatoes.* In 1998, he began presenting the National Lottery show on Saturday night on BBC1, and made the news again when Madonna appeared live on British television for the first time in more than a decade.

That same year, he paid tribute to his old friend and erstwhile stand-in Kenneth Williams when he hosted a tribute to the great man, and he also appeared in a tribute to Larry Grayson. And, as well as starting to present *Points of View,* he was to be seen in such diverse productions as *The Talk Show Story* and *Battle of the Fantasy Bands.* He might not have been quite as omnipresent as he had been until recently, but there was still a fair amount of Terry on the box.

It was time to relax. Terry talks so much about how easy his job is – if it can be called a job at all – that it is easy to forget quite how hard he has worked. His presence everywhere required a lot of effort, something Terry has always played down, but by this stage in his career he could be said to have earned a rest. And he had a hinterland. Terry's life was not entirely taken up with his work: he had a wife and family he doted on, his golf, houses in various countries and the wherewithal to lead a very pleasant life. His was one of the most successful careers on television and radio. Why not take it a little bit easy now he had more time?

And, despite the odd moments of grouchiness, Terry continued to do the odd full-time series. *Wogan's Web,* which was broadcast in 1998, was one: it ran only throughout May that year but has become something of a cult classic among viewers. The show went out at lunchtime and featured many of the characters who were also on Terry's radio show: his producer Paul Walters, with 'Deadly Alancoat' providing a voice-over and Tel's Belles on phone duties.

The format was similar to the radio show: although there were guests, much of the programme was made up of banter between Terry and his colleagues, reading emails and larking around. Only 20 episodes were ever made before the series was brought to a halt. There were whispered suggestions that the show was taking listeners from Jimmy Young on the radio, and, if this was true, it may have been why *Wogan's Web* had such a short run.

In fact, there has been more than one attempt to transfer the spirit of Terry's radio show to the television, and it has never really worked. Part of Terry's genius as a broadcaster is to create a little world his listeners can visualise and so it's always slightly spoiled if anyone tries to put it on screen. The television shows that have suited Terry best have always been completely different from his radio work and in their various individual ways have matched another aspect of his wide-ranging abilities.

But there was nothing like the successes of yesteryear, no *Wogan* or a new *Blankety Blank.* It is hard, with that kind of success under your belt, not to hanker in some way after past glories. This might explain the grouchiness, although it is at odds with Terry's assertion that he really doesn't care about the future of his career. He does, of course, and why shouldn't he? Terry was one of the biggest names in British broadcasting throughout the last quarter of the 20th century, so it would be surprising if he didn't feel a bit grumpy about the fact that he is doing nothing like it now.

He is, however, doing something else. And it is something that has been growing in popularity ever since he started it, to the extent that he is as famous as ever and as big and important a presence in broadcasting as he ever has been. That something else can be heard from Monday to Friday between 7.30am and 9.30am on the radio, and these days at least eight million people tune into it. For, in 1992, after *Wogan* was axed, Terry decided to return to his first love. He went back to Radio 2.

8

WAKE UP TO WOGAN

In many ways, it was a return home. Terry Wogan, probably the most popular presenter Radio 2 has ever had, was on his way back to the medium that had made him famous. He was to take over from Derek Jameson on the breakfast show, his old stamping ground, on Radio 2. In the wake of the demise of *Wogan* on television, he might have been feeling disillusioned with that particular brand of presenting, but he was still very much appreciated in some quarters. He had only given up his breakfast show in the first place in order to present *Wogan,* and so the bosses at Radio 2 astutely realised that this was the moment to get him back again. And they did.

Terry himself was delighted to be coming back to the place that held so many happy memories for him. He recalled the day when he took up the breakfast show again. 'I remember the very first one when I was asked to do it,' he said. 'I came in early and the studio was down in the basement. I arrived at seven o'clock, and sat on the floor outside the studio for 20 minutes, waiting for somebody to come and open it. Ever since then, I don't come in any earlier than five minutes before the thing is supposed to start.'

And that set the tone from the start. If he didn't do any preparation for *Wogan,* he did even less for the radio show, preferring to treat each day as it came. And, while there is absolutely nothing amateurish about Terry Wogan, that is somehow the image he managed to convey: the genial old geezer who somehow has found himself in front of the microphone in a radio studio. His image is summed up perfectly in the logo seen on many sweatshirts sported by his fans, which reads: 'Do I Come Here Often?'

His fans were overjoyed. There were many who were still missing him from the first time round on the radio show: to them, it seemed as if Terry had simply taken a prolonged break from the microphone and was coming back to where he really belonged. The stage was set for what has been, to date, nearly a decade and a half of merriment. There are many who feel that Terry's is exactly the right tone with which to start the day: irreverent, sarky – a little man bewildered by a big world. Terry was back on the radio, and in some quarters, at last, service could resume as normal.

Given the massive success he has enjoyed on television, it would be inaccurate to say that Terry's best performance comes from behind the radio mike. But, according to Terry himself, it is certainly where he feels most comfortable. He has often said that appearing in front of a huge audience has sometimes been an ordeal for him, and that he feels nothing like the airy nonchalance that he exudes.

He says that he has a fundamental shyness, an element in his character that, like everything else, he is able to laugh about. 'Nobody minds admitting to being shy,' he says. 'Not too many people say, "Actually, I'm tremendously bombastic and egocentric." Nobody admits to that. So, shy is good.' It's certainly not what the public think about Terry, but it may well inform his style of broadcasting.

In those early days of 1993, it was also a chance to rebuild his career. For all that he claimed hardly to notice where his career was headed, he had been badly wounded by the events surrounding the end of his television show and this was a chance to prove himself once more. And there is no doubt at all that he had been badly treated by the BBC. Terry was one of its greatest assets, had brought in viewers by their millions and had taken a great personal risk when he began fronting that show: even if it had been time for it to come to an end, he should have been treated with a great deal more dignity. His increasingly frequent outbursts against the BBC are proof that the wounds inflicted at that time exist to this day.

Another possibility that had been under discussion was to move *Wogan* to a weekly late-night slot, but the BBC had decided against this also. Terry was none too thrilled with the way any of it had been handled. 'The BBC made such a mess of it – they knew I was going to make the change for more than a year,' he said. 'That was really a sore point with me.'

To add insult to injury, the TV presenter Mike Smith had publicly declared that, had it been up to him, he would have kept *Wogan* the show but ditched Wogan the man. Terry was measured in his response. 'If you knock somebody more successful than yourself, it always looks like envy,' he said. 'If you knock somebody who's less successful, it looks like bullying. So it's best to keep your mouth shut.'

Smith had also very publicly applied for the job of BBC programme controller. Terry managed to be diplomatic about that too. 'He'd probably be a lively choice, but I don't think he's got much chance of getting it,' he said. 'I've always been very nice to him. I'm sure he just had a rush of blood to the head. My only response to Mike Smith is I hope he gets my job! I'll try to hang on as long as possible!'

On that other delicate topic, judging whether he had allowed himself to be spread a little too thinly, Terry was equally unruffled. 'People used to say to me, "Do you think you are overexposed?" But you are never overexposed if the public finds what you are doing is acceptable,' he said. 'The Nineties is a new ball game and we'll see if I can stay precariously perched on the Matterhorn. The thing is, if you are going to slide, you've got to make your slide imperceptible. Go down slowly, sideways!'

And, back on the radio, he was in his element. 'Radio gives you a perspective that television can't,' he said. 'You get such a feedback on radio in terms of mail and response.' There had been some initial doubt as to whether Terry should return to breakfast broadcasting: some people saw it as a comedown from the lofty heights of prime-time television. It wasn't, as Terry himself was well aware, but he was also aware that other people thought differently.

It is odd that no one has ever tried properly to replicate the phenomenal success of his radio programme on television. As mentioned in the previous chapter, there have been attempts to move the programme to TV, but they haven't worked because, for the breakfast show, the best format is radio. What the BBC should do is look at Terry's listenership, take on board their other likes and dislikes and learn from that. It could also do a lot worse than listen to Terry's preoccupations, given that he acts as a sort of barometer of middle-class, middle-aged tastes. That would bring back the giant audiences of yesteryear, but it is unlikely that anyone is going to have that kind of common sense.

Terry himself is fully aware of this. Asked in recent years if BBC bosses should learn from the success of Radio 2 and start aiming towards a slightly different audience from the one they are currently courting, he replied, 'Nobody in BBC Television ever notices BBC Radio, and people in BBC Radio resent BBC Television. There's a mistaken idea that we're both working towards a common end. It's not that way. There's an understandable jealousy between the two sides.'

Of course, back in the beginning, it had been seven years since he had last broadcast on the breakfast programme, and in that time Terry himself had changed. With age comes acceptance of who we really are and a greater degree of self-awareness, and Terry was not immune to the insights brought by the passage of time. 'I used to think I was quite intelligent, but the older you get, the more you realise you're not,' he said.

'You see, what I do, you can either do it or you can't. And I'm lucky, I can do it. So it doesn't take a lot of effort. Quite often in my life I've done things and thought, If I'd put a bit more effort into that, it would have been better. But I have no capacity for taking pains. I'm there to do a job and so I do it. And it's probably indicative of my basic shallowness that I love doing it.'

What was actually the case was that he had found what he excelled at. It would be a big mistake to see Terry as shallow: there is much more thoughtfulness behind the public image than he usually lets on. Terry was once asked if his blitheness was actually a form of defence, just as some of the greatest comedians use humour to stave off the unhappiness of the world. He was having none of it. 'What you're really saying is, "Do you not ever stop and think, What am I doing? Is this what I was made to do?" But you can't stop and think about that too much, because you'd never get going then. You have to find something and do it. If you start intellectualising, you're going to be very unhappy.'

But there is more self-analysis, more self-awareness going on than he likes to make public. There has to be. Terry has been asked so frequently about the secret of his success that he has been forced to ponder the issue. He has written an autobiography and is preparing a second book, which of necessity takes some inward searching. But, above all, there is the unanswerable question: why him rather than anyone else? Radio and television are overflowing with talented people: why was it Terry who made the grade in the first place and has hung on so long while others have not lasted the course? Talent, luck – and an indefinable ingredient – all have played a part here.

Once back on the radio, Terry found that he did not actually miss *Wogan* at all. It was, after all, very hard work: drawing people out and getting them to talk about their lives is not as easy as it looks. Doing it on live television three times a week is more onerous still. Terry had had his fill of it: there was only relief now that the show was part of the past.

Many years later, shortly after he appeared as a guest on Parkinson's newly revived chat show with Martine McCutcheon and Jennifer Lopez, he said, 'Martine is ideal – talks like she's at her own fireplace. But when J.Lo came on, I thought, Thank goodness I am not still trying to do this. The answers you get are so predictable and formulaic.'

And so he set out to win Britain over once again. Nor did it take long. Terry's salary has always been a closely guarded secret, but it was estimated by this time to be about £500,000, making him one of the country's best-paid presenters. But, indubitably, he earned it. Radio 2 has never had the reputation of being 'must talk' radio, but the new show became popular almost immediately. He also won the Sony Radio Award in 1994 for the Best Breakfast Show. Terry's future was assured – again.

Not that there hadn't been other opportunities for him to consider. In 1993, when the BBC was looking for someone to fill the role of programme controller, Terry revealed that he had been asked from time to time to follow that kind of path. 'I could have produced my own shows if I had wanted to, but I've never wanted to get into the business of producing as well as performing,' he said.

'In general, I would say the last five years have been lousy for the BBC, but they are coming out of the woods now. I want to see [as programme controller] someone who is in contact with his people. That is the essence of management.' Terry had always been in touch with his people too, but it was a wise decision. His best work comes about when he is allowed a free hand: to have to operate under all the constraints of senior management would almost certainly have hampered his style.

As the years have gone by, two things have happened. On the one hand, Terry's style, not just on the radio but generally, has become seemingly out of synch with modern times. In other words, he's old-fashioned. At the same time, however, he's continued to gain listeners hand over fist, ending up with the biggest radio audience in the country. So, old-fashioned is what people actually want. Terry may not be flashy young showbiz, but he is what people tune into.

He himself is aware that times have changed. At an industry dinner a few years ago, he related that he was taken aback by all the whooping and shrieking that went on. 'Our business isn't about projecting beyond the camera or the microphone,' he said. 'If you look at what goes on in children's TV, everybody is in your face, behaving as if they are projecting for the back row of the stalls. You think, Hold it down to a dull roar and you may be OK. But you have to be terribly careful, because anything that you say that is even mildly critical means you sound like an old fart. And you probably are.'

In more recent years, his future has become an obsession. Absolutely determined never to repeat the experience he had with *Wogan,* Terry is determined not to hang on for too long. Retirement and when to go is a constant topic in interviews: if nothing else, it certainly concentrates the minds of the Radio 2 programme controllers, who would find him an act that was almost impossible to replace. 'Will I have the guts to retire?' he said on one occasion. 'What you have to avoid is leaving with a bad taste, hanging on too long. But what is too long?'

These days the last thing the BBC wants is for Terry to retire. There is no one else at all who could possibly bring in the kind of audience he does, and he knows it. It would be vulgar to say that he has the BBC over a barrel – but he has and the amount of time he wants to spend with his radio show is unquestionably a matter for him to decide. And, if one were minded for revenge, this one is sweet: the organisation that publicly humiliated him when his television show came to an end is now the very same one that is desperate to keep him at all costs. He could walk into a job with any rival and, as for the financial aspect, he has been so well paid for such a long time that there cannot be any need for him to work a single day more for the rest of his life.

But Terry continues to tease both his listeners and the BBC. Will he go or won't he? How long will Radio 2 really get to keep its national treasure on the air? Terry never misses an opportunity to waft the possibility of his departure past an awful lot of very anxious noses. Not that it would be just a matter for him: his wife would have a say in it too. And Terry is unsure how Helen would take to having a husband who is around all the time.

'She has developed a social life of her own,' he says. 'She's better than I am socially. In my job, you work with three people. You don't get to build up a whole new set of friends. I don't think she'd welcome my stopping at home. But the BBC air conditioning is not good for your health. If you don't come out with Legionnaires' disease, you're extremely lucky.' This is slightly disingenuous. The couple enjoys a very active and happy social life together, but Terry never misses an opportunity to point out that one day he might really not be there.

In fact, age seems to have affected him in many different ways. For a start, it's made him less tactful and less tolerant than he was in earlier years. Because he has nothing left to prove and is set up for life several times over these days, Terry is not afraid to speak out and upset people. For such an avuncular figure, he has been remarkably outspoken in recent years, especially about the BBC. Very few presenters would be allowed such licence. But more about that later.

He has also mellowed. On that extremely prickly topic of religion, Terry is beginning to take a softer line than he has done for years. Having said he'd never return to the Catholic Church, he began to imply that, however remote, it was a possibility after all. 'Well, people do tend to come back when they're looking for the exit,' he said, in an uncharacteristically gloomy moment, but even that would have been an unthinkable thing to say several years earlier.

He might have been openly critical of his Jesuit education, and once confided that his mother believed it was the Jesuits who made him lose his faith, but then he does talk about them an awful lot and frequently refers to himself as a product of the Jesuits. For him, a return to the Church might not be as unlikely as he himself once believed. 'A belief in God is a great consolation to people,' he said on another occasion. 'It's a possibility when I lie on my deathbed that I'll say a few prayers just in case.'

In 1997, the first recognition of what he had really achieved in his career came when he received the OBE. Then, in 2004, he received another award with kudos: an honorary doctorate from the University of Limerick. Terry really was part of the establishment now, and he was good-humoured about it, taking the mickey out of himself. He was a member of the Garrick Club, one of the most exclusive establishments in London, but it was something he tended to play down when it was commented on.

'So I am a member of the establishment,' he said, when an interviewer pointed out that he was wearing the Garrick's distinctive salmon-pink and cucumber tie. 'The Garrick has a lot of old fogies and when I get there I think I must be the youngest member. It's a wonderful building with some magnificent paintings. But I'm the worst member of any club of which I am a member. I rarely go to the golf club; I rarely go to the Garrick.'

Golf actually has played quite a role in Terry's life: one great friend is Peter Alliss, another target of

Terry's teasing ways. 'I never had a word of advice from my great friend Peter Alliss, no matter how many times I've played with him,' he said. 'No, I tell a lie: Alliss did, once, offer me encouraging words. "Give it a crack," he said. Which just goes to show how much he knows about amateur golf. Give it a crack – the pill would fly off at right angles, probably, decapitating the lady captain five fairways away!'

On another occasion, he spoke about belonging to his local golf club. 'I play little, I reckon it must cost me on average about £500 a round,' he said. 'Helen plays a few times a week. Golf is not an obsession. We had a wonderful time on the celebrity golf programme. During Treaty 3000 we hosted my charity tournament in Limerick.' It is a pastime that suits him, and one that many of his listeners also have a taste for. In his recreational pursuits, as in so much else, Terry is at one with his audience.

And, if anything testifies to becoming a member of the establishment, it is becoming so famous that you are mentioned in song. Exactly that reward was Terry's when he was referred to in 'The Dark of the Matinee' by Franz Ferdinand. 'So I'm on BBC2 now telling Terry Wogan how I made it,' they sang. Terry's reaction is not known.

While Terry might be more publicly outspoken than he once was, his home life has become more contented than ever. Terry and Helen have been married for so long, and weathered various family storms, of which more in the next chapter, that they are more at ease in their lives together than they have ever been. 'I give Helen breakfast in bed on Saturday and she gives me breakfast in bed on Sunday,' he says. 'Generally, I don't get up on Sunday until about half-past one. We are just Darby and Joan. Sometimes we might go out for lunch on Sunday, but we usually stay at home as Helen is a wonderful cook.'

Terry remains a great reader, and says that, while he may not be religious, he is spiritual. 'I read a lot,' he says. 'I am interested in religion, in philosophy, in why people believe what they believe. And I love poetry.' His favourites are Gray's *Elegy,* Edward Thomas's 'Adlestrop' and Robert Frost's 'The Road Not Taken' and 'Stopping by Woods on a Snowy Evening'.

And he has continued to fret about when would be the ideal time to pack it all in. 'I probably will not continue beyond the extent of my next contract, because that is the restrictive element in my life,' he said in the late 1990s. 'And I think anyway the laws of diminishing returns will set in. You can't continue rising forever. Since I came back to Radio 2, it has grown and grown to become the biggest radio station in Britain, with the most listeners, and my morning show has the biggest listenership, with about six million. It is very successful, but nothing keeps rising on a never-ending curve. The last figures show that I have added a further quarter of a million listeners. But at six million, you are probably as close to a ceiling as you will achieve. So I feel there is another two years at Radio 2, provided that I am well, healthy and enjoying it.' It was yet another reminder to his Radio 2 bosses of his worth – and, of course, he did stay on, winning a further two million listeners to date.

That outspokenness continued to grow. In 2000, Terry caused a sensation when he published his autobiography, *Is It Me?.* It was a strangely self-effacing title, implying a degree of insecurity that he certainly didn't always show, but what really got everyone's attention was his description of his schooldays and an attack on the BBC. His comments about his Jesuit education and the reaction it provoked have already been covered here, but equally blistering were his remarks about the BBC.

In an excerpt published in the *Radio Times,* no less, he hit out at the Beeb's sports coverage, and in particular *Grandstand.* He accused the BBC of adopting the maxim 'If it ain't broke – break it'. He went on to say that the Corporation worries more about 'carpets for middle-management offices' than holding on to sporting rights. '*Grandstand* is now a joke. Rallying and bowls, with curling to add some spice during the winter.' He then turned his attention to Radio 5 Live, commenting, 'You can always fiddle the figures.'

There was absolute outrage at his remarks. Terry was, after all, a BBC grandee – practically the public face of at least one part of the Corporation, and there were some people who simply could not believe that he of all people could be, as they saw it, so disloyal. What many had forgotten is that Terry had been on the receiving end of some pretty heavy-duty disloyalty himself. He had never forgotten or forgiven what had happened to him some years earlier and this was in some ways settling the score. Not that he saw it like that, of course – he was merely saying what was on his mind.

The row raged on, but Terry was entirely unrepentant. 'Ah well,' he said. 'You can occasionally say the odd word about where you're working and surely anybody can say what they like about the BBC. We all pay licence fees. I've always perceived the BBC as a place, not a fascist organisation – a place where anybody can express an opinion. For some reason – I think it's because the organisation is in a period of transition – certain heads of department have overreacted, when they would normally have said, "What does old Wogan's opinion count for?"

'There's Michael Heseltine's autobiography coming out this week and – well, perhaps he should have said something about the BBC! Old hobbledehoy says a couple of well-meaning words and the next thing ... Ah well, the BBC will survive me. My opinions on the BBC were hardly meant to wound. The fact that some people got wounded perhaps tells you more about them than it does about me. I'm not saying anything which isn't said all over the BBC or, indeed, by 99 per cent of the listeners. So there's no point in getting in a huff and jumping up and down. The reason is probably they feel a bit vulnerable and they think they have to stand up and show the new boss [Greg Dyke] that they're at the coalface.'

But some people within the BBC itself were livid. 'If Terry Wogan has such a problem with the BBC, which, after all, has given him several of his own TV series, his own radio show and no doubt an excellent salary – funded by licence payers like me – then why is he still here?' asked Stuart Murphy, head of programming at BBC Choice. 'Wogan is sounding out of touch, out of date and seems to be living in the bizarre fantasy world of an *Auntie's Bloomers* script. What arrogance to get the BBC to pay him to publicly criticise what we are doing. Wogan should feel free to have a private chat with me about BBC Choice in case he wishes to air misinformed views about the TV channel I run. It may help if I explain to him about digital television and the future in general.'

Terry could not have been less perturbed. 'Mr Murphy is entitled to his opinion as I am entitled to mine,' he said smoothly. 'I am a freelance broadcaster and the BBC employs me because I bring in an audience of seven million every morning, which is probably more than Mr Murphy delivers in a year. I wish him luck with BBC Choice and hope he gets more viewers. I loved my years working for the BBC and I have really enjoyed them.'

His real feelings became clearer on another occasion, when he caused yet more upset by saying that he had no special feelings for the Beeb, and would have been perfectly happy to move to Sky. 'The BBC only uses you while you remain popular,' he said. 'To have loyalty to a big corporation is madness, you are going to get a broken heart.' That strongly suggests that Terry's heart had been a little bit broken some years earlier – otherwise his hostility might not have had such an edge.

His remarks certainly put the cat among the pigeons. So much attention was paid to them, and indeed the rest of the book, that Terry was asked to appear at Edinburgh's Festival Theatre, where he was to be interviewed by the television presenter Mary Marquis. She professed herself delighted to be meeting the great man for the second time. 'He won't remember me, but we have met before, way back,' she said. 'After I'd done a *Good Morning Scotland* stint I staggered into the canteen and we exchanged only a few words as we confronted the burned bacon and congealed eggs.

'No, he doesn't know who I am, but I greatly admire him as a broadcaster and his communication skills. You can hear his voice as you read the book, especially at the start, where he describes growing up in Limerick. He pokes fun at the BBC in the book and, yes, you can see he is disenchanted, too. Well, anybody who's been with a corporation as long as he has knows its failings and its good points. While the reading is whimsical, he doesn't miss his targets.'

Other members of the Wogan family also continued to flourish. Over in Ireland there was some excitement when it emerged that one Paula Wogan, 22, had made it to the top five on a programme on RTE called *Selection Box.* This was the Irish version of *Popstars* and it was Paula's father, Brian, Terry's younger brother, who had urged his daughter to apply.

'I never had any intention of pursuing this kind of career, but I went along to see what it was all about,' she said. 'I wasn't nervous, because there were so many people I never imagined I would get anywhere.' Her elder sister Jane was branching out into show business too: after posing for the men's magazine *Maxim,* she landed a job fronting a holiday programme on Channel 5.

Very wisely, Terry continued to guard against believing his own publicity. As he reflected on his career, he continued to maintain that it was all down to good fortune – and even sounded a little wistful as he did so. 'People who are successful should never forget that it's 90 per cent luck,' he said. 'You've got to be an eejit to be an egomaniac. I had my glory years – *Blankety Blank,* the talk show, when I was winning every award going. But now half the population doesn't know who I am.'

He did, however, win a Sony Award for the show in 2002, an honour he addressed with his characteristic modesty. 'Just because someone votes for you as the greatest thing of its kind this century doesn't mean you have to believe it,' he says. 'You also know that there are millions of people out there who, if they had the same opportunity, could do the same thing. It isn't brain surgery. It's a very small – "talent" is too big a word. But it's great. I love it.'

His attitude to himself had become refreshingly simple over the years. One of the comforts of ageing is that most people genuinely care considerably less about the impression they make on other people, and Terry is no exception to that rule. Why should he be when he has had the kind of success of which others can only dream? 'As far as I am concerned, people can make up their own mind,' he said.

'If they don't like me, they don't like me and that's fair enough. I don't come from a showbiz or theatrical background. I did not come from the concept of going out on stage and entertaining people and making them laugh. I've never had the nerve – and, in a funny way, the inferiority complex – to go out on stage and make people love me.'

Despite this frankness, however, there has always been a side to Terry that is utterly impenetrable and private. It has been one of the secrets to maintaining his equilibrium and sanity throughout a life that has been, in part, so very public. Terry never made the mistake of baring his soul to anyone, not even when his autobiography came out. He might have been openly critical of some institutions and individuals, but he never gave a true glimpse of what was lurking at the bottom of his soul.

'You only give away a bit of yourself,' he said. 'Nobody gives all their heart away. It would only get broken if you did that. Everybody keeps a little of themselves behind. You have to do that, because, if the real you came out, you would get stoned in the street.' Nor does that barrier ever come down. Interviewers have often remarked that, while he had been genial and friendly in their company, they never got down to what was the *real* Terry. The thoughtful aspect of his character has become more marked.

But it seemed as if he simply couldn't resist continuing to bait the BBC. It made headlines every time he did so, which did nothing to make him hold his tongue. 'Morale is not good,' he said a year or so after his autobiography came out. 'As for the preposterous idea of funding it through voluntary contributions: if that ever came to pass, it would be dreadful. If they take away the licence fee, it would be all over.' On another hot issue, he expressed his distaste for 'This extraordinary mantra of appealing to "yoof" as if youth were a specific section of society that never grows older.'

This was a subject that he was to return to time and again, but the fact is that he's right. Terry and his middle-of-the-road programme get massive audiences; cutting-edge alternative characters do not. Nor does the fact that he's growing older himself matter to anyone – Terry has simply grown in popularity, just as he has in years. He has a seemingly unbreakable bond with the rest of the public and he is entirely right to take a swipe at the BBC about its all-consuming obsession with youth.

But there is one aspect of Terry's life that this book has only touched on so far, and that is his children. At the time of writing, they are all hard-working, personable characters, but a few years ago that was not quite the case. Terry has had problems with his offspring, just as any parent does, and in his case the dramas had to be played out in the glare of the spotlight.

Indeed, he once said that he wished he'd adopted a stage name, so that his children wouldn't be recognised by their famous surname. It's too late for that, but all are happy, healthy and a joy to their parents – now. There have been some bust-ups along the way, though, as we'll see in the next chapter.

9

TERRY, HIS CHILDREN AND GABY ROSLIN

One of the most important aspects of Terry's life, and the one that is probably the least reported on, is his family life. All three Wogan children are now grown up and two of them are married, but family remains at the absolute centre of Wogan's existence. In the background, he has always had Helen, with whom he has a rock solid relationship, and the children, Alan, Mark and Katherine. All three have turned out to be a credit to the father they adore.

Right from the start, Terry and Helen were aware of the pressure their children would come under, growing up with such a famous father. The fact that they didn't actually live in London must have helped. Out in the countryside they were shielded from the excesses and extravagances of the celebrity lifestyle that has often wrought such havoc on children of the famous. All were healthy and happy children, and life, when they were young, was secure.

Terry was an easy-going father and Mark, the middle child, once related that he and his brother Alan were only ever smacked once. 'We had a very liberal upbringing,' he recalled. 'I can remember Dad hitting us only once. He said he felt so awful afterwards, it wasn't worth it. We've both been grateful for Dad's support financially, although he doesn't throw his money around. If you misused it, he would come down on you like a ton of bricks. He's also very good on guidance. I count him as one of the wisest men I know – he's never let me down yet.'

Certainly, the children have happy memories of growing up with their famous father. Given how important home and family was to him, they clearly benefited from their father's presence and speak warmly of their life at home. 'Home was always incredibly important to him,' Katherine, the baby of the family, once said, 'and after doing the *Wogan* show for the BBC three times a week he'd always rather come home and have dinner with Mum than go out to the many functions he was invited to.'

Mark was as warm as his sister in recalling the early days: 'It's hard to fault Mum and Dad as parents,' he said. 'Of course, when we were younger, they did what they thought was best and we did what we wanted to do, but somehow, without being excessively strict, they managed to instil respect in us.' It is a quality that has informed the lives of all three children and in Mark's case was very possibly the attribute that helped him when he had a brief patch of trouble later on (see later in this chapter).

Wogan was a very hands-on father and certainly made it his business to be around. 'I used to see my kids a lot when they were little because I'd be back in time to pick them up from school,' he said. 'Katherine would always say, "Park the Rolls as far around the corner as you can." I think I embarrassed her. We always had our meals together; we were a great family for meals. And on birthdays, the whole family has to come together and everybody has to spend too much on presents. That's my wife's fault – she gives a lot of presents so she's ruined everybody. We always overdo it. Christmas is ludicrous. I'm always trying to have cutbacks, but nobody listens.'

Presiding over the whole household was the gentle presence of Helen, who is the focal point around whom the family revolves. She had not entirely given up work when she married Terry and continued to do the odd job even after Alan came along, which simply enthralled her family even more. 'Mum did all the Paris shows and went on modelling into her thirties after she'd had Alan, my elder brother,' said Katherine. 'And yeah, she's beautiful, "St Helen of Taplow" we call her. She's so gentle, kind and generous – everybody loves her.'

Normal as their childhood might have been, the Wogan children were always aware that their father was a famous face. And it was not only Terry's children who were aware of what their father did, it was everyone else they knew, too. Right from the start life was different because, unlike anyone else in their village, they had a famous father who appeared on television every night.

'We all used to watch *Wogan,*' said Katherine, 'but he'd never want to talk about it and when he got in, we'd say, "Oh, good show, Dad." He'd say, "Yeah, it was all right." And that was it – it was just something he did. But my friends would want to talk about it the next day and that would piss me off. I'd get questions like, "Is your Dad as funny at home as he is on TV?" And I was like, "Yes, he's hysterical." It wasn't really something that I particularly wanted to talk about. And friends would ask, "So how does he deal with such and such?" And I'd be thinking, don't ask me – he's my Dad and that's as far as it goes!'

Of course, they had to deal with a certain amount of stick for having a famous father but they learned to manage when they were still young. 'I always managed to cope with the fame thing,' said Katherine. 'I was like Dad in that I wouldn't react to it. But yeah, I got stick – I used to get called "Bogey Wogey" and people would heckle me on the train to school. I'd just laugh because it was pathetic.

'But I used to think, shut up! Once or twice I lost it and grabbed someone by the scruff of the neck. But I've always had a group of friends that I trusted so I wasn't isolated by it. It makes you much more cautious about friends because you always wonder, "Do they want to know me because of who my father is?" – I can spot that a mile off, always have been able to.'

And Terry had taught them to cope. 'Dad always taught me that if I was teased to just walk away and they'd get bored eventually,' said Katherine. 'I've always just kept to a small group of friends that I can trust implicitly, probably because of that. You have to have a certain defence mechanism, be slightly more wary of people – I think you grow up a good judge of character.'

Otherwise, though, the family was as normal as it could be under the circumstances, with the usual rows and scuffles when the children would squabble amongst themselves. 'We got on very well but we had big rows too, at which point Alan would usually intervene,' said Mark, remembering his relationship with Katherine as a child. 'Katherine was very strong-willed and would always speak her mind although she had the capacity to see what was wrong – eventually.'

'I was definitely the annoying little sister,' said Katherine. 'But when I got to the age of 16, my brothers began to see me as a person rather than as some object they could bully and hit so I started to socialise with them.' She was growing up into quite a looker, too. As an adult, her looks have been compared to those of Meryl Streep and she was beginning to come into her own.

But no family gets off scot-free and the Wogans were no exception. Mark was the one who was to have a short brush with trouble. Alan became the head boy at his school and went on to university, while Katherine also took a degree. But Mark was different. He was less academic than the other two and more prone to slightly worrying behaviour, and he was to cause serious worries for his parents while he was still young.

He was 'politely asked to leave' two of the schools he attended and there was further upset when, aged 15, the police discovered him walking in a daze on the hard shoulder of the M4. It must be said that this happened at exam time, a time when many adolescents come under a great deal of pressure, and had his father been anyone else the episode would probably have gone unnoticed. However, it was the first of several events involving Mark and a sign of further upheaval to come.

As an adult, he is adamant that any subsequent problems he had were nothing to do with his famous father. Indeed, to his credit, Mark took all the blame himself. 'I know everyone thinks I've been the victim of my father's name,' he said. 'But to tell you the truth, I've never found it a great burden. I learned to live with it at school. Boys used to ask me what it was like, having a famous father. I'd say it was OK – he was just Dad to me – he doesn't go around bragging about being a star. He doesn't even bother watching himself on television.' It was a telling tribute to the way the parents had brought the children up.

Mark's biggest problem, however, surfaced at the height of Terry's fame, in 1989. It emerged he had become something of a heavy drug user, a habit he first started at his school in Basingstoke, when he began to smoke dope. 'It was the thing to do – like saying, "Hey man,"' said Mark, a couple of years later. 'I thought it was being part of the scene, I didn't think it was wrong – and I never considered it would lead to harder drugs.'

But it did. After leaving school, he went on to get a job as an insurance broker at Lloyd's of London and left home to live in a flat on Chelsea's King's Road. He was a young man about town with all his life ahead of him and, as so many people do in that situation, he messed up. It was then that his habit began to get out of hand. 'I was living on my own in Chelsea but I wasn't lonely,' he said. 'I had lots of friends and I went to parties all the time. I was thrilled out of my mind with it all – it was bright lights and the Big City. My lifestyle stepped up, it was moving faster than ever before. I was working all day and doing things all night; that was the routine.

'It was so different to the college I'd gone to in Henley, where all we did was mess around and have a few beers,' he said. 'And, of course, the temptation to take drugs was intensified. Suddenly I realised that everything was available. I discovered that hard drugs were as available as soft drugs had been at school. If you're a young person around that scene, it's only a matter of time before it's offered to you.'

And so the real problems began. 'Your first hard drug is like having your first cigarette, or your first drink,' he said. 'It's new, it's exciting. I snorted cocaine for the first time at a party and yes, it did make me feel good; it gave me a terrific high. I thought, I've arrived, I was part of the Chelsea scene. I think I even started bragging that I was having far more than I was. I wouldn't have dared to say it then, but to tell you the truth, I'd really rather have a drink than snort a line of coke.

'Later I went to another party and was offered something much stronger – Ecstasy. It was difficult to refuse because everyone in the room seemed so happy. They seemed to be saying, "Look, we're having a fun time – try it." So I took this little pill they gave me. I remember thinking one won't hurt me – I'll just give it a go. Within half an hour I experienced this overwhelming feeling of euphoria. It lasted five, perhaps six hours; I felt fantastic. Then, suddenly I began to feel frightened. I looked around at the others. Something in my brain told me, "This isn't a good time, this is fake good time."'

It was the wake-up call he needed. Not only was the experience a shock, but something of an epiphany, too. Mark was adamant he had never used heroin and never taken drugs at the family home, but he was aware that his life was careering out of control and this habit had to be stopped – now. And so he decided to take it on the chin and wrote a letter to his parents telling them the truth and that he had now put a stop to his potentially lethal habit.

'It left me with no hangover,' he explained. 'But I was stricken by conscience. It's such a powerful drug, I knew people could get hooked from just one pill. I thought, how is it affecting my mind? What will it do to me? Then I had the worst thought of all, what would Mum and Dad think of me if they knew? I knew I wasn't as bad as I could be, I'd never be tempted to try heroin – that's a killer. Heroin's a loser's drug – I swear I'll never take it. But I'd got as far as snorting cocaine and trying Ecstasy. I knew I had to stop before it was too late.'

Mark's confession was a dreadful shock to Terry and Helen. 'Of course, we were devastated,' said Terry. 'We're just like all parents. I worry about my kids all the time. I'm always asking them, "Are you all right? Are you eating OK?" If they're in London, I tell them, "I hope you're not indulging in any foolish practises." But though we were shocked at Mark's news, we were also proud of him. Hel and I both know that soft drugs can lead to hard drugs, and that hard drugs can kill you. But at least he told us the truth and risked our wrath.

'We think it takes real guts to do something like that and we're proud he was man enough to do it. If you have three children and two never put a foot wrong, but one's a bit wild – well, that's not too bad, is it? No family in the world goes through life without traumas. And though I'm famous, we're really no different from all other families. I appreciate that Mark wants to take total responsibility for his own mistakes.'

Mark continued to maintain nobly that his famous surname had nothing to do with what had gone on. But unlike his son, Wogan did feel his celebrity had made him a target. 'To some extent at least, I believe he is a victim of my fame,' he said. 'There are always going to be people who want to ingratiate themselves with the children of the rich and famous, and that can lead to them being introduced to the drugs scene. Mark certainly isn't the first celebrity's son or daughter to fall victim and he certainly won't be the last. As parents, you can only hope that your children have the strength to cope with their own lives and the fact of their father or mother being in the public eye.'

This was not, however, the end of the story. After the drug revelations, Mark returned to the City, but soon found it was not entirely to his taste. 'I tried the City and hated it,' he revealed some years later. 'When I went to work for Lloyds as an insurance broker I thought I was in with a chance of making some serious money – you know, all those stockbroker types with big piles in the country – but it didn't really work like that.' He was not alone: at the time the City held an allure for a great many young people who subsequently decided their preferred career lay elsewhere.

And so he decided to change track completely and dabbled briefly in public relations before retraining to become a chef. He also became a manager in the music industry, which added yet more to his CV as he had also worked in a menswear shop ('15 quid for a Saturday, horrible'), as a builder and as a barman. He was clearly finding it difficult to decide on the industry in which he would make his mark.

It did not help that, like so many before him, he discovered that deciding to give up drugs and then actually doing so was not quite so easy as it seemed, and he quietly slipped back into his bad old ways. Some years later, however, at the age of 22 – by which time he was running a catering firm – Mark decided, again, that something had to be done. This time he was determined to succeed.

'I wasn't a particularly happy person,' he said, some years after he'd finally kicked the habit. 'I just wasn't happy with where I was going. Taking drugs began as a social thing but it started to encroach on my life. I wasn't doing drugs day and night, and I never perceived myself as a junkie. There's a fine line between going out, partying and having a good time, and it was becoming a problem. I felt I was crossing that line and I didn't want to go any further. There came a point when I realised I needed help – I was 22, 17 stone and miserable. I didn't want to be like that anymore. I had professional help and was lucky to have a lot of people who gave me support. But at the end of the day, you have to take responsibility for yourself.'

This time round he managed to stay clean – so much so that he put his experiences to good use and became a counsellor at The Priory, the famous London hospital specialising in problems such as drug abuse and depression. This allowed him to justly feel proud of what he was doing with his life.

'It's not something I wanted to be made public, but the press had seen me going in and out, and rang a friend of mine to ask if I was receiving treatment,' he said. 'And, of course, it was exactly the opposite. I get a lot out of it. When you count yourself lucky that you've got over something such as drugs yourself then it's important to give something back. If you don't then you never fully appreciate how lucky you've been.'

It was around this time that Mark decided that he was interested in a television career. He, more than anyone, was well aware of the double-edged sword his surname provided. On the one hand, he might get the odd job offer, but on the other he'd always be subject to the charge that he'd used his father's name to get on. Then, of course, there was a further problem: if he fell flat on his face, he would do so under the full glare of the media. In the event he actually did very well, presenting a programme on

Sky and working on *This Morning,* but it was still a high-risk strategy. 'Dad's a tough act to follow,' he said with commendable understatement, 'and people are always going to draw comparisons. You know, "He's only got that job because of his old man," that kind of thing. But at least I know that's not the case.'

He started his television career at the very bottom of the heap, which was probably a wise move. 'My first job in TV was as a runner, which was mainly making the tea, and I was paid about £200 a week,' he later recalled. 'It's a funny business. Some people make a fortune, but at the lower end of the scale it's a starvation wage.'

Nonetheless, he soon found that he enjoyed what he did. 'I had perhaps subconsciously steered away from it for obvious reasons but I realised it was what I really wanted to do,' he said of his new career. 'I never used the nepotism card because I think the Wogan name would have closed down as many doors as it opened. About six months after I joined *This Morning,* someone said to me, "We all expected you to be a wanker." So I was starting on the back foot without knowing it.

'If I became successful under another name it would not take people more than about five seconds to work out who my father is. Then I'd be asked if I changed my name because I was ashamed of my father. I'm actually proud of him, so why would I shun the name? And the thing that has made me proudest is that he and my mother managed to bring up a happy, close family within an industry that doesn't necessarily always allow that to happen.'

Mark's first big job – in a Channel 4 series called *Here's One I Made Earlier* – made use of his training as a chef. He then moved on to *This Morning* and *Sky.* He was now well paid for his pains, but admitted that to earn it was to spend it. 'The problem is that I'm numerically dyslexic,' he said. 'I struggle to keep track of how much I spend and I do enjoy spending – I am a passionate believer in the power of retail therapy.'

Katherine, meanwhile, had become an actress. Initially, she had gone to the University of Madrid, after which she attended Manchester University to study languages. She worked briefly as a translator before taking to the boards and touring the country with local dramatics companies, although she had done some acting before – in conjunction with the British Council – when she was in Spain.

Her first real break came in 1998 when, aged 25, she was chosen to play the role of Mary, Duchess of Richmond, in the BBC series *The Aristocrats.* It was the London agent Barry Burnett who spotted her and he was enthusiastic about his new find. 'We just thought Katherine would be perfect for this role in *The Aristocrats* and the producers thought the same. She has an innate talent,' he said.

Katherine herself was thrilled with the role. 'She's not very nice, really,' she said. 'She's the sort of character who takes malicious delight in other people's misfortunes. She comes in, raises an eyebrow, says something sarcastic and leaves – it's such fun to be able to play a bit of a cow like that.' In the event she acquitted herself well and went on to appear as Clare Costelloe in *Grafters* the following year on ITV, for which she received great acclaim.

All three of the children remain close to their parents. 'People think it's quite strange because we all see each other as often as we can – for instance, at least one of us children will always go home for Sunday lunch,' said Katherine, several years ago. 'We also spend New Year and birthdays together, and the five of us try to go on holiday together once a year. I recently went on holiday with them for a week and spent the entire time with them – I don't know many girls of my age who could do that with their parents.'

Not that theirs was a remotely serious household. Terry painted a boisterous picture of life chez Wogan. 'My mother had a wit like a razor and Katherine is like her,' he said. 'She's a lovely laugh. She laughs at my wife – "Silly old tart," all that kind of thing. And of course they laugh at me because I'm turning into an old fart. If I'm making a noise when I'm eating or something, there's a lot of jeering. My wife is always wiping bits of crumb off my chin and accusations of dribbling go on – Katherine really enjoys all that.'

As the years have passed, Wogan's family has caused him great joy. Mark was the first to take the plunge. In 2002 he announced his engagement to Sue Acteson with the wedding set to take place in the Wogan's home near Albi, in France. 'I proposed over dinner,' said a slightly flustered Mark immediately afterwards. He was by now working as a chef in London's Groucho Club, alongside doing more television appearances.

'It came as a complete surprise, but she said yes straight away. We haven't set a date for the wedding yet, but it will be next year.' Friends approved – Mark was now 31 and it was time to settle down. 'They look great together,' said one. 'Terry's mansion in France is so large it even has its own chapel, which would be ideal for the ceremony.'

The legendary closeness of the Wogan children was to kick in again. Where Mark led, Katherine followed. Just a few months later in 2002, aged 27, she became the second Wogan to announce her engagement: in this case to Henry Cripps, the eldest son of Judge Michael Cripps. Henry will one day inherit a title – that of Lord Parmoor – which means that like her mother, Katherine will be a Lady one day.

Back at work, however, Wogan continued to seek out new challenges. In 2002 he had been seen in the company of the wild man of radio, Chris Evans. After a 12-month long honeymoon with the actress Billy Piper, Evans had recently returned to the UK and was casting around for new projects. He felt, rightly, that not enough was being made of Terry's talents on television and that with a suitable vehicle, he'd get him back on air as much as he would have been in his heyday; the trick was to find the right kind of programme.

Another performer Evans considered underused was Gaby Roslin. He had worked with her on *The Big Breakfast,* the two had stayed friends and Chris respected her as a performer. And so it was that *The Terry & Gaby Show* was launched on Channel 5 in June 2003 at 11am, the slot it was due to fill, on and off, until March the following year. It was launched with the intent of taking on *This Morning;* something, sadly, that it never managed to do.

In retrospect, of course, it is easy to work out what the problems were right from the start. The first concerned energy and timing. One of the reasons why Wogan decided to do the show was that he wouldn't have to give up his breakfast programme on the radio as he had had to do when *Wogan* was on primetime TV. However, it didn't seem to occur to anyone that this meant he would finish broadcasting *Wake Up To Wogan* at 9.30am in Broadcasting House. This is on the north side of the Thames, which meant he only had an hour and a half before going on air at Five's headquarters on the south side, so it was stretching him that little bit too thin.

The set-up was this: Terry and Gaby would sit on a sofa, chatting away to their guests, while amusing letters and emails from viewers were read out in the course of the show, just as they are on *Wake Up To Wogan*. What works on radio, however, is not always right for TV. Their guest on the first day was the ever-reliable Jonathan Ross, while Johnny Ball popped in for a daily slot although eventually, and with no explanation to the viewers, he was replaced by Danny Baker. This made for a certain lack of consistency that may have put people off.

Another gripe was that despite the show's title, one of the two star presenters always seemed to be away on holiday. Guest presenters, including Les Dennis, Lionel Blair, Jimmy Tarbuck, Richard Whiteley, Linda Barker, Jenny Powell and, on Children in Need Day, Donny Osmond, were brought in but where this had not seemed to matter back in the days of *Wogan,* now it did. The show never quite settled in people's minds as a piece of television and, because of those frequent absences, Terry and Gaby never seemed to set up an onscreen partnership in the way some TV presenters do.

Another problem was the combination of the Evans/Wogan broadcasting styles. They might admire each other as professionals, but they were oil and water. And so the show contained elements that were pure Evans – a slot called 'Kids in Headphones', for example. This involved a young child singing along to a song on his headphones and if the viewers identified it, they won a prize. It wasn't really very Terry. Another slot, 'Live Loot', involved a running gag in which Danny Baker was given £100 to go around buying items from people's houses to give away on the show – this, too, sat ill with Terry's surreal musings on life.

Nor was he particularly interested in the guests. On his radio show he admitted he hadn't a clue who the previous day's guest had been. This was hardly a ringing endorsement of the show that was to once more bring him to the forefront of light entertainment. Indeed, he was visibly bored by some elements. During the Danny Baker give-away segment, he was seen to wander off in search of a drink of water before gazing morosely out of a window with some justification. Initially the programme had been commissioned for 200 episodes, but at the end of the run it was not re-commissioned.

If truth was told, Wogan didn't seem to care. He had nothing to prove and he certainly didn't need the money. Although he never confirms the figure, the BBC is believed to pay him £500,000 a year for the radio show, but in this, as in so much, he is keen to emphasise his good fortune. 'I've been very lucky,' he said. 'All my life I've worked in something that I love and it happened to reward me well, so I've had it both ways. Anyone who is successful and has made a bit of money, if they don't realise how lucky they are, then they're fools.'

He has been very canny, too. Talking in 2003 about his finances, he admitted he'd cashed in many of his investments before the stock market crashed. 'I felt that the stock market wasn't going to go on rising indefinitely,' he explained. 'I had a lot of pensions. Mercifully, and in my shrewdness, I've taken them all. I've avoided the ridiculous and disgraceful penalties that have been imposed on people of my generation who put money into pensions and then found that the amounts of money they were supposed to be getting have been cruelly diminished.'

Another slightly rueful subject was Ireland itself. His relationship with his homeland remained rather a sore point: he was so utterly anglicised there was no question of going back. However, he continued to speak of Ireland as you would a family member: you're allowed to criticise but no one else can.

'I've never had any patience with the Irish people who've been here for about 45 years and still say, "I'm going home for the summer,"' he said. 'I think that has been our problem here – the Irish immigrants that went to America realised they were never going back, so they flung themselves into the politics and all the rest of it. But we've not yet realised the full extent of our power in the UK. Maybe one day we will, or maybe we don't need to now.

'When I left Ireland, the main thing you would notice was the national inferiority complex. There were certain things like greeting the visitor by saying, "What do you think of Ireland?" Australians do that as well – it's a sign of a slight inferiority complex. But when you come over to England, no one gives a monkeys what you think of the place!'

But life had changed in Britain, too. Wogan had come to the country during the hugely exciting 1960s. Four decades on and the picture looked very different. Like many men of his age, he could be pretty disillusioned with what he saw going on around him, not least when it came to falling standards in public life. 'I don't think the cream of intelligent life decide to be politicians any more,' he said on one occasion. 'As soon as they get into the Commons, they're in the hands of the Whips. They don't vote the way of their conscience, they do what they're told.'

The BBC is another to incur his wrath. 'BBC TV gets hold of an idea and beats it to death until we're all heartily sick of it,' he said. 'They buy people without thinking what they're going to do with them. It's the wrong way around. What they should be doing is employing really good ideas people to come up with good ideas; that's what they used to do at the BBC.' Indeed he was to comment that the only BBC signing he agreed with over the last decade was that of Jonathan Ross.

His irritation is understandable. For years, the BBC kept Wogan tied to them by means of 'golden handcuffs'. It was back in 2001 that the Corporation, with typical malevolence towards those it no longer regarded as a favourite son, allowed it to 'become known' that he had been released from his golden chains. But Terry took it all on the chin. 'Everybody gets shafted by television in the end,' he said. 'It's like all the England football managers are doomed to abuse in the end. I look at Sven-Goran Eriksson and I think you're having a wonderful honeymoon now, but when Germany beat us it will be back to Turnip-ville. And it's the same thing with television. When things finish, as they're bound to do, you have always been axed.'

Once he'd started, though, it seemed he couldn't hold back. 'The penny has finally dropped for the BBC,' he said in 2004. 'You're making programmes for people who aren't there. They've been aiming at the wrong market on Friday and Saturday nights – yoof, aged 15–35, which is what advertisers like. But on Friday and Saturday nights the yoof are in pubs or clubs.' Next to feel the heat was reality TV, which he seems to hate even more. 'We've had this ridiculous *Hell's Kitchen,* where people who can't cook are supposed to produce food,' he said. 'What's the point? It's more vulgarity, it's encouraging the public to sneer at poor pseudo-celebrities. It's demeaning, it's futile, it's awful.'

And for him *Big Brother* was even worse. 'Reality TV is a downward spiral,' he said. 'In the end we're going to end up with – well, we've already ended up with soft porn – but hard porn. That's the only way it can go; it can only go down the sexual route because we've had everything else – the arguments, fighting and jealousies.' As ever, he was right.

10

THE TOGMEISTER RUFFLES FEATHERS

'Chinese scientists have calculated that Everest is four inches shorter than we thought. We are all doomed!'

TERRY WOGAN

These days it has its own website: www.togs.org – 'an online home for the bewildered'. Its adherents often wear a T-shirt bearing a particular slogan that reads, 'Do I come here often?' They meet once a year at an annual convention and between times they communicate via the Internet. They are 'TOGs', or Terry's Old Gals or Geezers, and Terry himself is known as 'The Togmeister', the beneficent leader of this most gentle and unassuming of cults.

Even calling them a cult is going too far. First, because Terry has 8 million listeners, every one of whom is in some sense a 'TOG' – which is a bit on the large side for a cult – but also because these are the people who have taken Wogan's life philosophy of never taking anything too seriously on board. And he and the TOGs have a connection no other DJ has with his or her audience, one that explains his phenomenal radio success: he knows exactly who he's communicating with, while the TOGs feel he's part of the family. It is a relationship that suits the various millions involved down to the ground.

Wogan's personality might be perfect for the show but, all talk about lack of preparation aside, he is the absolute, consummate professional. His listeners want something cheerful and that is what they get; he never allows personal feelings of any kind to set the tone for the day. And he knows how to cope with down moods, too. 'You learn over the years not to try too hard when you're not feeling well because it sounds false,' he once said. 'I was born an optimist, I can put aside hurt and pain when I work – that's the difficult thing in what I do – the rest is easy. I don't indulge myself in the luxury of bad moods, this is what I do.'

The show about which all the fuss circulates has been honed and refined into possibly the most successful radio programme ever to go on air. Its producer is Paul Walters, or 'Paulie', the heartthrob for Terry's Old Gals and it is he who enables the connection between Terry and 'TOG' to be immediate. During the course of the programme up to 600 emails come in and Walters filters these down, getting rid of the mundane and the unpleasant, before passing about 100 on to Terry himself.

Of these Wogan chooses about 60 to read on air, imbuing each one with that sense of the absurd that has set him so far ahead of any rival. A web camera watches over the show and posts images onto the BBC website, which in turn provokes immediate TOG response. On one occasion, when Walters put up a shot of the studio engineer, Graham, wearing shorts, emails started to come in almost immediately: 'Whose short, fat, hairy legs are those?' 'It's comfortable here in Cardigan Country,' said Terry, beaming affably into the microphone. This is a world in which unpleasantness is banished, mild eccentricity encouraged and nothing ever, ever taken too seriously. It is a world designed for the comfortable middle-aged.

And yet Wogan's listeners are not simply the middle-aged and over – many of his most devoted fans are very young. For what he has really created is a world that never really existed, one that harks back to yesteryear when certainties seemed a lot more certain than they are now, when society was a kinder, gentler and slower thing. No matter that it is the speed of today's communications that allows Wogan to have such immediate contact with his listeners; this man is the same small-town boy from Limerick, with all the values and goodwill that society seems to yearn for once more.

Wogan himself is very well aware of all of this. He refers to the 'good-natured recriminations' between the listeners and to the TOG motif itself as: 'A send-up of the mythology of ageism. Peter Allis epitomised it for me. He was commentating on the

Ryder Cup. He said, "There he is, Jose Maria Canizares, 41. He walked around the course unaided."'

And, of course, Wogan himself is older now. His knighthood comes at the age of 68 and while it is almost unthinkable to call him old-aged, he is in his pensioner years. He and a substantial part of his audience have grown up together. Twenty years ago they were all obsessed with *Dallas* – these days, they've all taken to the new technology with gusto and spend their time emailing one another. Terry is not just the Togmeister but the *pater familias,* the grand old man presiding over a vast family, from the very young to the very old.

He likes his older listeners, though. Once asked why the programme was so popular, he replied, 'Because I'm the best – the others are all eejits. Also, I've been doing it the longest and daily broadcasting is all about familiarity and repetition. I think my reign will continue – as long as there are more old people in Britain than young people, I'll be OK.'

An atmosphere of mild hysteria can prevail. Asked about his worst faux pas on air, he sounded positively gleeful. 'Well, I make it up as I go along, so we'll have a faux pas a day,' he said. 'The most recent one wasn't particularly my faux pas. It was just that my producer broke wind while the microphone was open. Nobody could speak for about five minutes; nobody could breathe. There was a lot of what can only be described as hysterical laughter.' Of course, on any other radio show this could have been taken to be deeply offensive, but on Planet Wogan it was simply another of life's enduring little eccentricities.

Wogan's obsessions can change from day to day, not least as a reaction to what the listeners are emailing in. One moment it could be Torchy the Battery Boy – a sixties cartoon set off by a passing mention to Cher's voice – the next it might be Latin quotations. Then there are the ongoing motifs – 'It's all in the buttocks,' 'I'll put that in a glass case and throw sugar at it'. It all builds up the feeling of eccentricity combined with a private club. If you understand the jokes, you're in.

Another crucial element to the success of the show is that Wogan retains the common touch. He has never become starry, never put himself beyond the reach of the common man. 'He is always in touch with what people are watching, reading and listening to, and despite being a star you can sense he leads the same kind of life as all of us,' says Radio 2 controller Lesley Douglas. 'You just know that when he comes home, he puts on the TV and has the same conversation about *EastEnders* with his wife that we have with our partners.

'Also, everything he does is done with great wit and intelligence. He is one of the cleverest people I have ever met; there is an honesty about what Terry does that I think is very enviable. There is something about his turn of phrase and his observations that add so brilliantly to his raw material. But above all, what shines through in his shows is the genuine enthusiasm for what he does. Listening to him, you can hear how much he loves broadcasting. He enjoys it and is completely at ease doing it – and that's what sets him apart.'

Unusually for today's airwaves, Wogan has little in the way of cynicism about him. A questioning nature, yes, an inquisitive one, certainly, and a teasing one overall. But essentially, listening to him the feeling comes across that this is a good world. Like everyone, he has been through the mill but he's emerged largely unscathed. He does not insult his listeners' intelligence and neither does he depress them; he speaks to them as equals and they, in turn, in their droves tune in.

And then the music is what people actually want to hear. Asked if he was to blame for the current vogue in easy listening, he replied, 'So shoot me for playing music that only the public likes. If you're 15 I'm sure you like Garage and Hip-Hop, but the vast majority of the country is over 40 and that is why easy listening has become so big recently – people are older.

'I get a lot of credit for people like Jamie Cullum and Katie Melua – Jamie Cullum played at my daughter's wedding, that's why I'm biased in his favour. But I wouldn't say there was a mania for easy listening. It's a passing fad, there'll be something else along in a minute.'

Wogan is very well rewarded for his work. He continues to refuse to comment on his remuneration, but he does not, however, shy away from making the point that he is very well paid. 'This is an earner,' he said, a few years ago. 'If you don't know your own value, nobody else will. If radio is the most popular medium and I'm currently the most popular thing on it, then I have to be paid commensurately. I don't want to be lagging that far behind Chris Tarrant, you know.'

It is, he says, partly out of respect for his listeners that he won't say how much he's paid. 'I have never talked about it,' he says. 'Also, think about the people who provide most of my material – they're probably not making an awful lot of money and they're providing me with my script. Instead of all this fuss about me, what about my listeners?'

The listeners are, of course, extremely important to the show, but it is Wogan himself who is the glue holding it all together and, despite the decades now of wealth and celebrity, he refuses to change. Nor will he start taking up the kind of past-times his listeners would clearly disapprove of – physical fitness? A regular round of golf will be enough for that.

'I have to say, the present Mrs Wogan and I have toyed with the idea – since our children all have personal trainers – we thought, why should we be the only ones without?' he said. 'Because friends of ours, of our age, have got personal trainers as well.

And we thought would that be good? And then we thought, no. Because, and I may change my mind on this, I don't want someone turning up at seven o'clock of an evening just when I feel like a drink and my dinner.

'This obsession with fitness stems from America, where everybody's been so tremendously successful and glamorous they don't see any reason why they should die, and that's really what it is: staving off death. And I'm an optimist. I'm afraid I'm the kind of man who wakes up and if I've got a pain in my chest, I assume it's indigestion, not a heart attack.'

Like his listeners, Wogan found his greatest happiness in the domestic side of life. Helen's famed cooking was a cause for celebration, one of his greatest highs. 'The high spot of my day is always my dinner,' he said. 'I love food and Helen is a wonderful cook. She always takes the trouble and I always have a delight in eating it. If I ate everything I wanted, I'd be easily 17 stone because I'm a mesomorph – short legs, long body – a Celt.'

He loves the subject of food and will respond positively to any questions about his own preferences, as when he was asked about his favourite biscuit. 'I think a custard cream,' he said. 'I probably don't eat them as much as I used to, though. One that you are probably too young to remember is a little ginger number with a sort of foamy top with coconut on it. Mercado biscuits made by Jacobs in Dublin, you see, so you wouldn't have had access to them – that would be my all-time favourite.'

Terry is certainly something of a bon viveur. He likes the good things in life and is also keen on the wines that go along with dinner – as indeed, his lifestyle allows him to be. But, as befits his unpretentious persona, he will not allow himself to come across as a wine bore. 'I like red wine, undoubtedly,' he says. 'My father was in the wine business so I grew up with it. I know good wine from poor, but I prefer to drink it rather than talk about it. I have some expensive wines, some nice Burgundies, but we have a house in France, in the Gascony area, so we experiment with the local wines.'

He is also not averse to making a joke about it at his own expense. 'I'm a very good drinker, as indeed the present Mrs Wogan is,' he once said. 'We're very hardened drinkers and we can drink virtually anybody in the world under the table.' But this is also kept well within the Wogan boundaries: drinking is a part of living well rather than behaving badly. Bad behaviour of the type seen so often in celebrity circles these days is unthinkable chez Terry and Helen.

But, as he grew older, he was aware that he had to maintain his physique in a way that would not have bothered him before. After all, he was still a public figure and appearance mattered. Indeed, a great deal of speculation has centred on whether or not Wogan wears a wig – a subject he does not deign to grace with comment – but he was aware that he must keep his body intact. 'Actually, I've lost a bit of weight,' he once said. 'Helen is cutting down. She has, over the last year, eschewed butter and cooked more with olive oil. But I think it's probably wastage, it's old age. We all get a bit thinner as we grow older. Helen always says my bottom has gone. That happens to men, of course – women's bums get bigger, men's disappear.'

(Actually, on the wig front, someone once plucked up the courage to ask Terry what was really perching on the top of his head. It was one of the few times in his life when he appeared absolutely flummoxed. 'Well, the thing is,' he responded eventually, 'it's always seemed to me that if you're going to wear something on your head why would you tell anybody? *If.*' Others who have met Wogan report that there is a silver thread running through his hair these days, which does indeed imply that it's real, as does a bald spot towards the back of the head.)

Indeed, for all his insouciance on the subject, age was, and still is a subject he constantly comes back to. For many people ageing can be a shock and he was no exception, although he played it down when talking about it. 'Nobody wants to get older,' he said. 'As soon as you get to 60, aches and pains arrive, the body thickens. And you do dumpen down, really – I must be shrinking. Honestly, men get smaller; you eventually disappear. Talk to me in ten years' time and you'll find yourself talking to a small Irish dwarf, a leprechaun!'

Wogan is, however, wearing the years well. He looks after himself, he takes moderate exercise and staves off time as best he can. While he may not be getting any younger, his face shows the effect of an agreeable lifestyle, not an excessive one. Helen, too, has kept her looks: her appearance suggests an age decades younger than her years.

And he is, these days, pretty content with his lot. Wogan has had an extraordinary career, dominating either the small screen or the airwaves – and sometimes both – for most of his adult life. Beyond any shadow of a doubt he is the most successful broadcaster of his generation, and has been for decades. He has reached a state where, frankly, he doesn't care what anyone thinks of him and certainly, as far as television is concerned, he's happy to allow everyone else to take centre stage.

'It comes naturally to me, broadcasting,' he said. 'There's lots of things I've loved on TV but I don't do anything I don't want to now. I've done all the awards ceremonies. *Wogan* was great fun for the first six years. I don't want to talk to anyone again, probably as long as I live – I've talked to everybody I want to talk to, I've sat and been bored stiff, trying to get people to talk. But Eurovision or Children In Need, that's different – they'll have to drag me away screaming. I will not relinquish those easily, they'll have to shoot me. Eurovision is without flaw: it is magnificent in its stupidity – grandiose rubbish.'

As for his relationship with Helen, it has merely strengthened over the years. Whenever he has a chance Wogan waxes lyrical about his wife. 'She is still beautiful,' he says. 'Oh yes, I feel the same about her. In fact, I probably love her more now, I love my children more now – I'm getting old and soft, that's what it is. You do, you get sentimental. But that's OK, I'm happy with life. But I've always been happy – I've had that gift. I don't live to work but I really love doing the radio. I wouldn't get up at half five to do it if I didn't. But it'll have to come to an end, and it will not immediately, but I have to have a bit more time to myself.'

That is, of course, the next big decision: when will Sir Terry finally decide to really call it a day? It is not a time Radio 2 bosses are looking forward to, but one day it will happen and until it does he will keep them guessing all the way. March 2007 is one likely date, when his current contract runs out. 'I know one should never say never, but I hope I'll get off the beach before the tide goes out,' he said shortly before his knighthood was announced. 'I've had thoughts about it and I'm going to do another two years, and then they're going to have to shoot me. But there has to be a time when you say, "Well, it's very nice, thank you, but I think the public will have had enough." I'll be 68 by then, though I don't know what

I'd do in the morning. My wife is very worried – what will she do with me? She'll be tripping over me.'

But he was still very much in situ and as such providing an inspiration for the up-and-coming generation of DJs. Indeed, Jamie Theakston, 33, who was taking over the morning slot on Heart 106.2 from Jono Coleman said that all morning DJs should follow the lead of the more established greats such as Wogan and Jonathan Ross. 'DJs like Wogan and Ross are brilliant at knowing what their audience wants,' he said. 'Other DJs in that breakfast market, who tend to be white middle-class men of a similar age – Johnny [Vaughn], Pete and Geoff [on Virgin Radio], Chris Moyles – ignore their audience and talk at them rather than to them. They like the sound of their own voice. And they all sound the same, that shouty laddish schtick – it's old-fashioned. People have moved on from that *Loaded* way of doing things.

'Wogan and Ross have this understanding of their audience's expectations, as Jono did before me. It's a real art and it's definitely what I want to do. I'm the same age and from the same kind of background as Johnny and Moyles, but what they do is not what I aspire to. I want to talk to Heart listeners and not just at them. These things take a long time, though. The most successful breakfast hosts of recent years, like Tarrant, have done it for eight or nine years – I'm happy to stick in there for the long term.'

The rival radio stations hit back. 'That's Jamie's opinion but it's not one we think is right,' said a spokesman for Radio 1. 'The bottom line is we're massively happy with Chris.' Nor was Capital Radio too thrilled. 'The accusation of laddishness is unfounded because Johnny's audience is 55 per cent female,' said a spokesperson. 'We say, let's let Londoners decide.'

It was at this point, a sunny Friday in June 2005, when the news first broke. Across the land radios were being switched on, the nation was settling down to its tea and toast, and the scrape of cutlery against china creating Britain's usual morning chorus. All was well with the world: the weather was getting warmer, summer was on its way and the country tuning into the nation's favourite breakfast programme. It was being broadcast on Radio 2. And then, as the pips counted up to the news, a million spoons clattered onto a million tables as it emerged that one of the most popular entertainers in the country had been awarded a knighthood in the Queen's Birthday Honours list.

Terry Wogan, who had won over hearts by the barrel load since arriving in Britain from Ireland nearly 40 years ago, was going to receive a knighthood. He was to be Sir Terry Wogan – or, more accurately, Sir Michael Terence Wogan, though no one had called him by his first name for a very long time. 'I am surprised and delighted that Her Majesty has given me this honour,' he said. 'I hope I can prove worthy of it.' No one is in any doubt that he will.

He was still managing to ruffle plenty of feathers, however. The good people of Scotland were rather irked when, on a trip to Aberdeen, from where he broadcast his show for a special week of events called 'Sold on Song', Wogan professed to be less than impressed with Scottish cuisine. After asking listeners for suggestions as to what he should eat, the local bakery sent him 50 butteries, or rowies. 'It's like a mouthful of seaweed,' said Terry, after taking a bite. 'I'm sorry, but it is an acquired taste. Maybe they would be better with a bit of butter or perhaps a dash of marmalade? I am finding them a bit salty – it's like eating dried sea water.'

Cameron Ross of the eponymous firm was unperturbed. 'We listen to Terry every morning and thought he'd like a buttery,' he said. 'I'm sure he would grow to love them if he persevered.' Alex Salmond, leader of the SNP, possibly the world's prickliest man when it came to matters Scottish, also put his oar in. 'Any man who judges the Eurovision Song Contest can hardly be held up to be a judge of anything,' he snapped.

But Wogan was unmoved. As 2005 drew to a close, the newly knighted Sir Terry was able to look back on a very fulfilling year indeed, and also to allow himself a small sense of satisfaction at the reaction to the latest news emerging from the BBC. It had been announced that Davina McCall, best known as the presenter for *Big Brother,* was to be given her own chat show. Not only was she the first woman to present a primetime talk show on the BBC, but also the first person to present such a show in an early evening slot since Wogan himself had given it up, 14 years previously. The BBC professed to be delighted with its choice. 'Davina is a great choice because she has real energy and empathy – she knows how to put people at ease,' said a spokeswoman. 'If anyone was going to be the BBC's first female primetime chat show host, she's the one.'

But others were a lot more cautious. Presenting *Big Brother* is one thing, hosting an intimate chat in which you draw out the innermost secrets of the famous is something else. From some quarters came one particular question: why not choose Terry himself? Given how much time had passed, a good deal of the bitterness caused by his departure from his show had eased. It remained the case that no one, with the exception of Michael Parkinson, could have matched Wogan as a chat-show host when he was on top form. But no – a younger, brighter model was picked to host the show which, when it finally aired, proved to be an unmitigated disaster.

If Wogan felt like gloating, he was sensible enough not to show it. Besides, he had plenty of other things on his mind – for a start, the 2005 Children in Need Appeal which he presented, and where he was joined by Natasha Kaplinsky and Fearne Cotton. So successful was the show that it raised more than £17 million.

11

WOGAN: NOW AND THEN

It had to happen, really. As recounted in the previous chapter, both TV bosses and the viewing public had cause to change their minds about Wogan as a primetime television interviewer. With the benefit of hindsight, to say nothing of innumerable examples by other television interviewers of how not to do it, it was clear that he was one of the all-time greats. UKTV Gold made the obvious move and decided to put Terry Wogan back in the interviewer's seat, a move that was treated with typical self-deprecation by its subject. 'Will it be entertaining?' he was asked. 'No,' said Terry. 'Don't make that mistake.'

But this was an interview show with a twist. Instead of any old celebrity with a book, film or TV programme to plug, the programme was – along with new guests – to feature the very same people who had appeared in the original *Wogan* chat show, who were also going to examine footage of themselves 20 years previously. Given the circumstances surrounding Wogan's departure from the original show, it was a slightly sensitive area for all concerned. He himself admitted it might have been difficult for him: 'After the Wogan show finished, I said, "That's it, I don't really want to talk to anyone again as long as I live."'

But that had been a decade and a half previously and clearly he was ready to step back into the hot seat.

Of course, the new format was of particular interest. 'This was slightly different,' he said. 'It's the retrospective aspect that's the attractive thing as far as I'm concerned. What impresses me is the bravery of people who are prepared to come on and look at themselves 20 years ago and talk about if their dreams or aspirations came true, that's what makes it interesting to me.'

He was, however, very keen to play his own role in all of this down. By now he was well aware that it was far better to dampen people's expectations than to fail to live up to them. When asked how it felt to be a television interviewer once more, he was rather downbeat. 'I don't care,' he said. 'Interviewing isn't some archaic art, it's just a question of asking the right questions and hopefully you get the answers you're looking for.

'My own style is basically what I do on the radio, which is slightly tongue-in-cheek, looking for humour and trying to have a bit of a laugh. So we won't talk too much about bird flu or indeed the current situation in the Ukraine. I'm not going to be confronting people, challenging them and demanding to know their innermost secrets, I don't really do that kind of stuff. Old Paxman does that, and it normally leads to tears – dear old boy. I've been criticised in the past for doing interviews that are bland, but if you're confrontational, after a month you'll find you'll get no guests. So, you've got to try and be nasty to people? What's the point of that?'

Of course, as a veteran of the small screen, and with no need to work or to prove himself, Wogan was now very much in a position where he could call the shots. Rather surprisingly, one aspect of the old show that he absolutely refused to countenance again was something that had almost been a hallmark: guests patting him on the knee. That was completely ruled out. 'That whole business used to drive me mad,' he said. 'It was the most irritating thing of all time. Of course, increasing numbers of PRs would say to the guests, "Touch Terry's knee, everyone likes that." When I'd see a hand reaching out, a cold fear would come over me. For God's sake, get off!

'This time I'm going to make sure the seating arrangements are such that the guests are too far away to be able to reach me. We'll have a bit of a hug to start, but apart from that there will be no contact whatsoever. Well, perhaps another hug goodbye, unless it's been a really bad interview, in which case they'll probably storm off.'

Then, of course, there were the interviews themselves. Again, an old pro like Wogan had been through his fair share of awkward encounters in the past and he explained that he cringed as much as the audience when something went wrong. 'No, my threshold for embarrassment is too low for that,' he said, when asked if he thought it made good television. 'Instead I'm thinking, isn't this awful? But I've got to make the best of it, of course, and keep smiling because that's what I do. But that doesn't stop me thinking inside, you are a complete eejit. How dare you do this? Why did you come on the show if you're not prepared to talk?'

It turned out that he also had a certain number of regrets regarding the past, one involving a memorable encounter with David Icke back in 1991. It was, of course, one of the few occasions when Wogan was actually pretty nasty, when Icke remarked, 'The best way of removing negativity is to laugh and be joyous ... so I'm glad that there's been so much laughter in the audience tonight.' 'But they're laughing at you,' said Terry. 'They're not laughing with you.' Of course at the time this brought the house down, but he felt pretty bad about it afterwards. It was, after all, rather a cheap jibe that was more attributable to TV hosts à la Clive Anderson, who made a point of being pretty rough with their guests, than dear old Terry. And now, in an act of some magnanimity, Icke himself was going to appear on the new show to discuss the past.

'I don't know whether or not to apologise to him for that,' said Wogan. 'Although it got a huge round of applause, and I suppose it was relevant at the time, maybe I shouldn't have said it. I don't want to be upsetting anybody. His beliefs are entirely his and sincerely held. I think you've got to be kind – why be nasty? Only kindness matters.' This sentiment, nice as it was, didn't last. After Icke's appearance on the new show, Wogan reflected, 'I always felt slightly guilty, I thought it only fair to give him a chance to appear a little more sane, but in fact he was as mad as ever.'

He was pretty gentle with his guest and the approach paid off. In the event, the show was a great success, attracting the likes of Boy George, Twiggy, Christopher Lee and Ulrika Jonsson, and the series, to Wogan's great delight, was re-commissioned. 'I'm constantly amazed at the people who are willing to look back 20 years,' he said. 'I love this show – it's a great opportunity to meet old friends and make new ones.' His guest list was starry, too. The second series kicked off with Liam Neeson and Cilla Black, an old mucker of his. 'I like to think I was instrumental in launching her second career,' he said. 'She appeared on my BBC talk show and she was wonderful, hysterical. ITV promptly offered her *Blind Date.*'

Terry, on talk show TV, was back. But things were not entirely simple, for scarcely had he settled back to enjoy this new part of his life when an absolute furore ensued as details were leaked about how much various broadcasters were paid by the BBC. It emerged that he was on £800,000, the highest salary of all, although some people were quick to point out that Jonathan Ross, on a salary of £530,000 but broadcasting fewer hours, was actually on a higher pro rata rate of £5.64 a minute.

But Wogan was dismissive of this speculation. 'No, no, I'm making more money than anyone else in BBC Radio,' he said with a touch of slightly unfamiliar steel when this was put to him. 'There's a limit to what radio can pay. When you look at some of the people who have failed abjectly on television and what they're earning, I don't feel the least bit guilty. If you divide my salary by my 8 million listeners, I'm costing tuppence a fortnight. I feel OK about that.' And he was breezily cheery about his everyday routine. 'Half-five, I get up, make myself a cup of coffee, have a piece of fruit and my yoghurt with the little friendly bacteria, whatever they are,' he said.

The message was clear: Terry Wogan was king of BBC Radio, a status only helped by the fact that he had so recently met the Queen, who herself was known to be a fan. 'Years ago, I met her at a Palace reception and she cried, "Flab!"' said Terry. 'That was in the days when I was doing a thing called "Fight the Flab". Last time we spoke she said, "Ah, the TOGs."' She didn't come across and say, "Hello, Terry, I'm a TOG." She didn't need to. Namedropping about the way the Queen had heard various items on his radio show proved beyond all doubt that Wogan now had Royal assent.

Nor was his knighthood the only honour that he received at that time. Another was a Sony Gold Award for lifetime achievement. 'I'm very pleased, but I'm also aware that it comes on top of getting the knighthood,' said Wogan. 'These signals aren't very good, are they? Look, for God's sake give him the gongs, and that will be the end of him.'

He was, though, now 67 and in a position to look back on what he had achieved. Financially, of course, he had done remarkably well, with no major problems experienced along the way. 'Helen and I have always been comfortable,' he said. 'I like being able to go out for dinner and have holidays whenever I like. I like living in a nice house and having a place in France. But I've always told my children that I've failed because I don't have a private plane – I really do hate airports.'

Life had been pretty good all round. Wogan continued to praise his wife to the skies: 'Helen is wonderful,' he said in 2006. 'I'm a better person because of Helen. She embodies all the qualities you would expect: she's very beautiful, loyal, true and funny. She's a fantastic cook, a great mother and she likes a game of golf.' He was also adamant that he had never so much as looked elsewhere. 'Well, at work, I never see anyone, unless you count Ken Bruce dropping in to steal one of my doughnuts,' he added.

Wogan is now a grandfather – Katherine has a son, Freddie, while Alan and Mark have taken over the running of their father's personal management company. But his first child, Vanessa, has never been forgotten. 'There's been precious little sadness in my life,' he said. 'But our first child died, which was awful, of course. If she was born now with a heart defect then it would be fixed.'

He was also very protective of Mark. Well past his bad patch, he still works as a counsellor at The Priory. 'Mark didn't get chucked out of school,' he said on one occasion. 'He left. All his life, that's going to be picked up and thrown at him, but he's a terrific son, and the very opposite now. Very few families come through unscathed. It doesn't matter how charmed your life is. Whenever I hear people boasting about their children, I think, excuse me, I've had a family and I know that life isn't like that – no one gets it for free. Suffering someone else's fame is never easy for kids. My children didn't resent it, though, and I think perhaps it made them better, stronger people. Things were never horrible, really – it didn't last, it's gone now, and I hate talking about it because I don't like embarrassing Mark.'

But some old wounds rankled. Despite newfound success in his old job, he still brooded about the ending of the Wogan chat show the first time around. 'I regret that I let the BBC persuade me to do another two or three years,' he said. 'I did feel that they wanted to change things. They said they didn't, but all the time they were building this village in Spain.' He was referring, of course, to the disaster that took over his slot: *El Dorado.*

There was also the question of when he was going to retire from his radio show. Given its ratings, it seems unlikely BBC bosses would want him to leave any time soon, but they can be capricious. There was the example of Jimmy Young, who left the BBC after eventually deciding not to take up the offer of a weekend show instead of his daily lunchtime slot. 'I think it was because Jim's whole life was that programme,' said Wogan. 'Mine is not, but the BBC have to look ahead to whom they're going to get because I am not going to last forever. I'll be reluctant to let the programme go, of course. It's not the fame, and it's not the money – it's the joy of doing it.'

But there were wonderful memories from the old days, and one involved *Dallas.* Wogan was planning to get the cast on to his new show. 'Larry Hagman was always as mad as a box of biscuits,' he said. 'I remember him joining me at Royal Ascot for Ladies Day in his Stetson with the budgie feathers all around it. He brought with him a ton of fake $100 bills with his face on them. And Sue Ellen took her clothes off on the London stage as Mrs Robinson, didn't she? No, no, I didn't see her – I didn't want my illusions ruined.'

Despite his advancing years, he still has a great deal else on his plate. His numerous other obligations, especially Children in Need and Eurovision, continue to play a part in his life. On that latter subject, he was as cheerily disparaging as ever. Speaking about the 2006 contest he said, 'I'd love to see Daz [the British entry] score a few points but he's not going to win it on novelty because there are a lot of what can only be described as "novelty" songs in the contest. There's Klingons and orcs singing for Finland, Germans in cowboy hats ... so when Daz comes on with a rap and schoolchildren it's not going to be that outrageous.'

As for the contest itself, he commented, 'I have always taken a porky, light-hearted view of the Eurovision Song Contest because in my view you have to. It's a silly old thing but it's magnificent in its foolishness. Political voting is a reality. Maybe in ten years or so Belarus will no longer be afraid not to give Russia douze points, but we've a way to go and it might see me out before that happens. Every year I expect it to be less foolish, and every year it's more so.' And who would want to change that?

As for the future, what will be will be. Wogan's position on the radio is probably about as unassailable as anyone's could be, and as he has said, he still enjoys doing it because it's fun. But it is clear that he will not allow a repeat of what happened when his television show was axed: he is determined to go on his own terms at a time of his own choosing. The TOGs might be devastated, but even Terry can't go on forever. All his life he has worked and earned great rewards in the process, it is not surprising that he now wishes to enjoy what he has.

And behind the casual, self-deprecating man on public show, there is quite a different Wogan, a *pater familias* rather more serious than he usually gives away. Unlike so many modern-day celebrities, he has been sensible and has kept something of himself in reserve rather than revealing everything to the world. The world, in turn, has very much appreciated what they got of him. Arise, Sir Terry, the pleasure has been all ours.

BACK COVER MATERIAL

Terry Wogan is Britain's most-loved broadcaster. From the moment his voice hit the airwaves in the 1960s, his dry, laconic wit and wry commentary style instantly won him legions of fans. Over the years he has picked up countless industry awards, won numerous listener and viewer popularity polls, received an honorary doctorate and been awarded an OBE. Now this immensely loved and talented entertainer has received the ultimate accolade – a knighthood from the Queen.

From a humble background, Terry worked his way from a small Irish radio station to the BBC where he hosted the Radio 2 breakfast show to record audiences of nearly 8 million. He talked his way through ten glorious years there before his glitteringly successful transition to television.

His sardonic observations on the Eurovision Song Contest and his long-running talk show *Wogan* are now the stuff of television legend. In recent years Terry has triumphantly returned to rattle the ratings with his Radio 2 breakfast show *Wake Up To Wogan* and his new talk show *Wogan: Now and Then.*

Author Emily Herbert draws on the reminiscences of many famous friends and colleagues to create an authoritative and entertaining portrait of one of the funniest, lovable and most prolific broadcasters of our time, offering invaluable insight into all aspects of the man, his life and loves. A fitting tribute to a true star in the world of entertainment.

Printed in Great Britain
by Amazon

78013070R00147